NEVADA PHARMACY

MPJE COMPREHENSIVE REVIEW

SMITH GIBBS, PharmD

SECOND EDITION

This publication is for informational use only.

This publication is not intended to give legal advice. For legal advice, consult a legal professional.

This publication is not intended to diagnose, treat, or be construed as medical advice in any way.

Application of any information remains the professional responsibility of the practitioner.

The author does not assume and hereby disclaims any liability to any party for any loss, damage, and/or failure resulting from an error or omission, regardless of cause.

NAPLEX®/MPJE® is a registered trademark of the National Association of Board of pharmacy. This publication is neither affiliated with nor endorsed by the National Association of Board of pharmacy.

For more resources visit our website www.rxpharmacyexam.com

Table of Contents **Pages**

PART ONE

PART TWO

PART-ONE

PHARMACISTS AND PHARMACY

NRS 639.020

Creation; number and appointment of members.

- The State Board of Pharmacy, consisting of seven members appointed by the Governor, is hereby created.

NRS 639.030

Qualification and terms of members; oath; vacancies; grounds for removal from office.

The Governor shall appoint:

- Six members who are registered pharmacists in the State of Nevada, are actively engaged in the practice of pharmacy in the State of Nevada and have had at least 5 years' experience as registered pharmacists preceding the appointment.
- One member who is a representative of the general public and is not related to a pharmacist registered in the State of Nevada by consanguinity or affinity within the third degree.
- Appointments of registered pharmacists must be representative of the practice of pharmacy.
- Within 30 days after appointment, each member of the Board shall take and subscribe an oath to discharge faithfully and impartially the duties prescribed by this chapter.
- After the initial terms, the members of the Board must be appointed to terms of 3 years. A

person may not serve as a member of the Board for more than three consecutive terms. If a vacancy occurs during a member'sterm, the Governor shall appoint a person qualified under this chapter to replace that member for the remainder ofthe unexpired term.

- The Governor shall remove from the Board any member, after a hearing, for neglect of duty or other just cause.

NRS 639.040

Election of President and Treasurer; qualifications, employment, duties, and compensation of Executive Secretary.

- The Board shall elect a President and a Treasurer from among its members. The Board shall employ an Executive Secretary, who is not a member of the Board. The Executive Secretary must have experience as a licensed pharmacist in this State or in another state with comparablelicensing requirements.
- The Executive Secretary shall keep a complete record of all proceedings of the Board andof all certificates issued and shall perform such other duties as the Board may require, for which services the Executive Secretary is entitled to receive a salary to be determined by the Board.

NRS 639.050

Meetings; quorum; salary of members; per diem allowance and travel expenses of members and employees.

- Meetings of the Board which are held to prepare, grade or administer examinations are closed to the public.
- Each member of the Board is entitled to receive:

- A salary of not more than $150 per day, as fixed by the Board, while engaged in the business of the Board; and
- A per diem allowance and travel expenses at a rate fixed by the Board, while engaged in the business of the Board. The rate must not exceed the rate provided for state officers and employees generally.
- While engaged in the business of the Board, each employee of the Board is entitled to receive a per diem allowance and travel expenses at a rate fixed by the Board. The rate must not exceed the rate provided for state officers and employees generally.

NRS 639.060

Biennial report to Governor.

- Before September 1 of each even-numbered year, for the biennium ending June 30 of that year, the Board shall report to the Governor upon the condition of pharmacy in the State of Nevada. The report must contain:
- A summary of the proceedings of the Board for the year.
- The names of all pharmacists registered under this chapter.
- A complete statement of all fees received.

NRS 639.065

Annual report concerning immunizations administered by pharmacists.

- The Board shall prepare an annual report concerning immunizations administered by pharmacists that includes, without limitation, the number of immunizations which were administered by pharmacists during the previous year, any problems or complaints reported to the Board concerning immunizations administered by pharmacists and any other information that the Board determines would be useful in determining whether pharmacists should continue to administer immunizations in this State. The report must be available for public inspection during regular business hours at the office of the Board.

NRS 639.067

Posting of information relating to pharmaceutical manufacturers on website.

- The Board shall post on a website or other Internet site that is operated or administered by or on behalf of the Board:
- A general description of the basic elements of the Compliance Program Guidance for Pharmaceutical Manufacturers that is published by the Office of Inspector General of the United States Department of Health and Human Services, or links to websites or other Internet sites that are operated or administered by or on behalf of the Office of Inspector General where such information may be obtained.
- A general description of the process for reporting unlawful or unethical conduct by pharmaceutical manufacturers to the Office of Inspector General, or links to websites or other Internet sites that are operated or administered by or on behalf of the Office of Inspector General where such information may be obtained.

NRS 639.070

General powers; regulations.

The Board may:

- Adopt such regulations, not inconsistent with the laws of this State, as are necessary for the protection of the public, appertaining to the practice of pharmacy and the lawful performance of its duties.

- Adopt regulations requiring that prices charged by retail pharmacies for drugs and medicines which are obtained by prescription be posted in the pharmacies and be given on the telephone to persons requesting such information.
- Adopt regulations, not inconsistent with the laws of this State, authorizing the Executive Secretary of the
- Regulate the sale and dispensing of poisons, drugs, chemicals and medicines.
- Regulate the means of recordkeeping and storage, handling, sanitation and security of drugs, poisons,medicines, chemicals and devices, including, but not limited to, requirements relating to:
    - Pharmacies, institutional pharmacies and pharmacies in correctional institutions.
    - Drugs stored in hospitals; and
    - Drugs stored for the purpose of wholesale distribution.
    - Examine and register, upon application, pharmacists and other persons who dispense or distributemedications whom it deems qualified.
- Charge and collect necessary and reasonable fees for the expedited processing of a request or for any otherincidental service the Board provides, other than those specifically set forth in this chapter.
- Maintain offices in as many localities in the State as it finds necessary to carry out the provisions of thischapter.
- Employ attorneys, inspectors, investigators and other professional consultants and clerical

personnel necessary to the discharge of its duties.

- Adopt regulations concerning the information required to be submitted in connection with an applicationfor any license, certificate or permit required by this chapter.
- Adopt regulations concerning the education, experience and background of a person who is employed by the holder of a license or permit issued pursuant to this chapter and who has access to drugs and devices.
- Adopt regulations concerning the use of computerized mechanical equipment for the filling ofprescriptions.
- Participate in and expend money for programs that enhance the practice of pharmacy.
- Enter into written agreements with local, state and federal agencies for the purpose of improving the enforcement of and compliance with the provisions of this chapter.
- The Board shall, to the extent feasible, communicate or cooperate with or provide any documents or other information to any other licensing board or any other agency that is investigating a person, including, without limitation, a law enforcement agency.

NRS 639.071

Regulations: Institutional pharmacies.

- The Board may adopt such regulations as are necessary for the safe and efficient operation of institutional pharmacies.

NRS 639.072

Regulations: Pharmacies in correctional institutions.

- The Board shall adopt regulationsconcerning the safe and efficient operation of pharmacies in correctional institutions.

NRS 639.0725

Regulations: Internet pharmacies.

- The Board shall adopt such regulations as are necessary for the safe and efficient operation of pharmaciesand wholesalers that offer their services to persons in this State via the Internet.
- For the purposes of this section, "pharmacy" includes any person who sells or offers to sell drugs topersons in this State via the Internet.

NRS 639.0727

Regulations: Remote sites, satellite consultation sites and telepharmacies; dispensing practitioners and dispensing technicians; practicing electronically, telephonically or by fiber optics.

The Board shall adopt regulations:

- As are necessary for the safe and efficient operation of remote sites, satellite consultation sites and telepharmacies.
- To define the terms "dispensing practitioner" and "dispensing technician," to provide for the registration and discipline of dispensing practitioners and dispensing technicians, and to set forth the qualifications, powers and duties of dispensing practitioners and dispensing technicians.
- To authorize registered pharmacists to engage in the practice of pharmacy electronically, telephonically or by fiber optics, including, without limitation, through telehealth, from within or outside this State; and
- To authorize prescriptions to be filled and dispensed to patients as prescribed by practitioners

electronically, telephonically or by fiber optics, including, without limitation, through telehealth, from within or outside this State or the United States.

NRS 639.073

Regulations: Restricting sale of drugs except under supervision of registeredpharmacist.

- If the public interest would best be served, the Board may adopt regulations restricting the sale of drugsto sale by or under the direct supervision of a registered pharmacist.
- Any regulation adopted pursuant to the provisions of this section shall also include the conditions underwhich such drugs shall be stored in a pharmacy and the circumstances under which such drugs may be sold.

NRS 639.074

Regulations: Registered nurses who participate in certain public health programs or provide certain mental health services.

- The Board may adopt such regulations as may be necessary to ensure that proper and adequate safeguards, including dispensing procedures, are followed to protect a registered nursewho:
- Participates in a public health program approved by the Board; or and that is operated by the Division of Public and Behavioral Health of the Department of Health andHuman Services.

NRS 639.074

Regulations: Transfer, security and exchange of information relating to prescriptions.

- The Board may adopt regulations concerning the transfer of information between pharmacies relating to prescriptions.

- The Board shall adopt regulations concerning the electronic transmission and the transmission by a facsimile machine of a prescription from a practitioner to a pharmacist for the dispensing of a drug. Theregulations must be consistent with inclusive, and the regulations adopted pursuant thereto and must establish procedures to:
- The practitioner and an insurer of the person for whom the prescription is issued.
- The pharmacy and an insurer of the person for whom the prescription is issued.
- Protect the identity of the practitioner to prevent misuse of the identity of the practitioner or other fraudulent conduct related to the electronic transmission of a prescription.
- The Board shall adopt regulations governing the exchange of information between pharmacists andpractitioners relating to prescriptions filled by the pharmacists for persons who are suspected of: Misusing prescriptions to obtain excessive amounts of drugs.
- Failing to use a drug in conformity with the directions for its use or taking a drug in combination withother drugs in a manner that could result in injury to that person.
- The pharmacists and practitioners shall maintain the confidentiality of the information exchanged pursuant tothis subsection.

NRS 639.075

Fiscal year.

- The Board shall operate on the basis of a fiscal year commencing on July 1and terminating on June 30.

NRS 639.081

Deposit and use of money received by Board; delegation of authority to take disciplinary action; deposit of fines; claims for attorney's fees and costs of investigation.

- Except as otherwise provided in subsection 3, all money coming into the possession of the Board must bekept or deposited by the Executive Secretary of the Board in banks, credit unions, savings and loan associationsor savings banks in the State of Nevada, or invested in United States treasury bills or notes, to be expended for payment of compensation and expenses of members of the Board and for other necessary or proper purposes in the administration of this chapter.
- The Board may delegate to a hearing officer or panel its authority to take any disciplinary action pursuantto this chapter, impose and collect fines therefor and deposit the money therefrom in banks, credit unions, savingsand loan associations or savings banks in this State.
- If a hearing officer or panel is not authorized to take disciplinary action pursuant to subsection 2 and the
- Board deposits the money collected from the imposition of fines with the State Treasurer for credit to the State General Fund, it may present a claim to the State Board of Examiners for recommendation to the Interim FinanceCommittee if money is needed to pay attorney's fees or the costs of an investigation, or both.

NRS 639.090

Enforcement of chapter; inspections.

- The members of the Board, its inspectors and investigators are designated and constituted agents for the enforcement and carrying out of the provisions of this chapter, and for this purpose they are entitled to have free access at all times during business hours to all places where drugs, medicines or poisons or devices or appliances that are restricted by federal law to sale by or on the order of a physician are held or offered for sale and to all records of sale and disposition of drugs, medicines or poisons or devices or appliances that are restricted by federal law to sale by or on the order of a physician.

NRS 639.093

Communication with other public agencies; immunity.

- The Board may communicate the results of its deliberations or investigations to other public agencies, and the Board or its members, agents, servants, employees, or attorneys shall not incur any liability as a result of such communications.

NRS 639.095

Board to furnish free copies of law and regulations to applicants and registrants.

NRS 639.097

Injunctive relief.

- The Board may bring an action to enjoin any act which would be in violation of the provisions of this chapter. Such action shall be commenced in the district court in and for the county in which the act is to occur and shall be in conformity with Rule 65 of the Nevada Rules of Civil Procedure, except that the Board shall not be required to allege facts necessary to show or tending to show lack ofadequate remedy at law or irreparable damage or loss. The action shall be brought in the name of the State of Nevada.

CERTIFICATES, LICENSES AND PERMITS

NRS 639.100

Unlawful to manufacture, engage in wholesale distribution, compound, sell or dispense drug, poison, medicine or chemical; exceptions; penalties; application for and issuance of license; Board prohibited from taking certain action regarding pharmacists located outside State.

- Except as otherwise provided in this chapter, it is unlawful for any person to manufacture, engage in
- wholesale distribution, compound, sell or dispense, or permit to be manufactured, distributed at wholesale, compounded, sold or dispensed, any drug, poison, medicine or chemical, or to dispense or compound, or permitto be dispensed or compounded, any prescription of a practitioner, unless the person:
- Sales representatives, manufacturers or wholesalers selling only in wholesale lots and not to the general public and compounders or sellers of medical gases need not be registered pharmacists. A person shall not act asa manufacturer or wholesaler unless the person has obtained a license from the Board.
- Any nonprofit cooperative organization or any manufacturer or wholesaler who furnishes, sells, offers to sell or delivers a controlled substance which is intended, designed and labeled "For Veterinary Use Only" is subject to the provisions of this chapter, and shall not furnish, sell or offer to sell such a substance until the organization, manufacturer or wholesaler has obtained a license from the Board.
- Each application for such a license must be made on a form furnished by the Board and an application must not be considered by the Board until all the information required thereon

has been completed. Upon approval of the application by the Board and the payment of the required fee, the Board shall issue a license tothe applicant. Each license must be issued to a specific person for a specific location.

- The Board shall not condition, limit, restrict or otherwise deny to a prescribing practitioner the issuance of a certificate, license, registration, permit or authorization to prescribe controlled substances or dangerous drugsbecause the practitioner is located outside this State.

NRS 639.120

Qualifications of applicants to become registered pharmacists.

An applicant to become aregistered pharmacist in this State must:

- Be of good moral character.
- Be a graduate of a college of pharmacy or department of pharmacy of a university accredited by the Accreditation Council for Pharmacy Education or Canadian Council for Accreditation of Pharmacy Programs andapproved by the Board or a graduate of a foreign school who has passed an examination for foreign graduates approved by the Board to demonstrate that his or her education is equivalent.
- Pass an examination approved and given by the Board with a grade of at least 75 on the examination as a whole and a grade of at least 75 on the examination on law.
- If he or she is an applicant for registration by reciprocity, pass the examination on law with at least agrade of 75.
- Complete not less than 1,500 hours of practical pharmaceutical experience as an intern pharmacist under the direct and immediate supervision of a registered pharmacist.
- The practical pharmaceutical experience required pursuant to paragraph (d) of subsection 1

- must relate primarily to the selling of drugs, poisons and devices, the compounding and dispensing of prescriptions, preparing prescriptions, and keeping records and preparing reports required by state and federal statutes.
- The Board may accept evidence of compliance with the requirements set forth in paragraph (d) of subsection 1 from boards of pharmacy of other states in which the experience requirement is equivalent to the requirements in this State.

NRS 639.127

Application for registration as pharmacist; payment of fee; submission of fingerprints;issuance of provisional registration; proof of qualifications; period of validity of application; issuance of certificate of registration.

- An applicant for registration as a pharmacist in this State must submit an application to the Executive Secretary of the Board on a form furnished by the Board and must pay the fee fixed by the Board. The fee mustbe paid at the time the application is submitted and is compensation to the Board for the investigation and the examination of the applicant. Under no circumstances may the fee be refunded.
- In addition to the requirements of subsection 1, each applicant for registration as a pharmacist shall submit with the application a complete set of fingerprints and written permission authorizing the Board to forward the fingerprints to the Central Repository for Nevada Records of Criminal History for submission to the Federal Bureau of Investigation for its report. The Board may issue a provisional registration to an applicant pending receipt of the report from the Federal Bureau of Investigation if the Board determines that the applicantis otherwise qualified for registration.
- Proof of the qualifications of any applicant must be made to the satisfaction of the Board and

must be substantiated by affidavits, records or such other evidence as the Board may require.

- An application is only valid for 1 year after the date it is received by the Board unless the Board extends its period of validity.
- A certificate of registration as a pharmacist must be issued to each person who the Board determines is qualified pursuant to the provisions of NRS 639.120, 639.134, 639.136 or 639.1365. The certificate entitles the person to whom it is issued to practice pharmacy in this State.

NRS 639.129

Payment of child support: Submission of certain information by applicant; grounds fordenial of certificate or license; duty of Board. [Effective until the date of the repeal of 42 U.S.C. § 666, the federal law requiring each state to establish procedures for withholding, suspending and restricting the professional, occupational and recreational licenses for child support arrearages and for noncompliance with certain processes relating to paternity or child support proceedings.]

In addition to any other requirements set forth in this chapter:

- A natural person who applies for the issuance of a certificate of registration as a pharmacist, intern pharmacist, pharmaceutical technician or pharmaceutical technician in training or a license issued pursuant to NRS 639.233 shall include the social security number of the applicant in the application submitted to the Board.
- A natural person who applies for the issuance or renewal of a certificate of registration as a pharmacist, intern pharmacist, pharmaceutical technician or pharmaceutical technician in training or a license issued pursuantto NRS 639.233 shall submit to the Board the statement prescribed by the Division of Welfare and Supportive Services of the Department of Health

and Human Services pursuant to NRS 425.520. The statement must be completed and signed by the applicant.

The Board shall include the statement required pursuant to subsection 1 in:

- The application or any other forms that must be submitted for the issuance or renewal of the certificate orlicense; or
- A separate form prescribed by the Board.
- A certificate of registration as a pharmacist, intern pharmacist, pharmaceutical technician or pharmaceutical technician in training or a license issued pursuant to NRS 639.233 may not be issued or renewed by the Board if the applicant is a natural person who:
- Fails to submit the statement required pursuant to subsection 1; or
- Indicates on the statement submitted pursuant to subsection 1 that the applicant is subject to a court order for the support of a child and is not in compliance with the order or a plan approved by the district attorney or other public agency enforcing the order for the repayment of the amount owed pursuant to the order.
- If an applicant indicates on the statement submitted pursuant to subsection 1 that the applicant is subject to a court order for the support of a child and is not in compliance with the order or a plan approved by thedistrict attorney or other public agency enforcing the order for the repayment of the amount owed pursuant to the order, the Board shall advise the applicant to contact the district attorney or other public agency enforcing the order to determine the actions that the applicant may take to satisfy the arrearage.

NRS 639.129

Payment of child support: Submission of certain information by applicant; grounds fordenial of certificate or license; duty of Board. [Effective on the date of the repeal of 42 U.S.C. § 666, the federal law requiring each state to establish procedures for withholding, suspending and restricting the professional, occupational and recreational licenses for child support arrearages and for noncompliance with certain processes relating to paternity or child support proceedings and expires by limitation 2 years after that date.

- In addition to any other requirements set forth in this chapter, a natural person who applies for the issuance or renewal of a certificate of registration as a pharmacist, intern pharmacist, pharmaceutical technician or pharmaceutical technician in training or a license issued pursuant to NRS 639.233 shall submit to the Boardthe statement prescribed by the Division of Welfare and Supportive Services of the Department of Health and Human Services pursuant to NRS 425.520. The statement must be completed and signed by the applicant.

The Board shall include the statement required pursuant to subsection 1 in:

- The application or any other forms that must be submitted for the issuance or renewal of the certificate orlicense; or
- A separate form prescribed by the Board.
- A certificate of registration as a pharmacist, intern pharmacist, pharmaceutical technician or pharmaceutical technician in training or a license issued pursuant to NRS 639.233 may not be issued or renewed by the Board if the applicant is a natural person who:
- Fails to submit the statement required pursuant to subsection 1; or
- Indicates on the statement submitted pursuant to subsection 1 that the applicant is subject to a court order for the support of a child and is not in compliance with the order or a plan approved by the district attorney or other public agency enforcing the order for the repayment

of the amount owed pursuant to the order.

- If an applicant indicates on the statement submitted pursuant to subsection 1 that the applicant is subject to a court order for the support of a child and is not in compliance with the order or a plan approved by thedistrict attorney or other public agency enforcing the order for the repayment of the amount owed pursuant to the order, the Board shall advise the applicant to contact the district attorney or other public agency enforcing the order to determine the actions that the applicant may take to satisfy the arrearage.

NRS 639.130

Reexamination.

- An applicant for a certificate as a registered pharmacist who has failed to pass the Board's examination for the certificate is not eligible for reexamination until the next regularly scheduled examination conducted by the Board.
- No subsequent examination may be given to any applicant until he or she has filed a new application and paid a fee therefor.

NRS 639.132

Board prohibited from approving application for registration or renewal of registrationas pharmacist or intern pharmacist unless applicant attests to knowledge of and compliance with certain guidelines related to safe and appropriate injection practices.

- The Board shall not approve an applicationfor registration or renewal of registration as a pharmacist or intern pharmacist unless the applicant for issuance or renewal of registration attests to knowledge of and compliance with the guidelines of the Centers for Disease Control and Prevention concerning the prevention of transmission of infectious agents through safe and appropriate injection practices.

NRS 639.134

Registration of pharmacist without examination; reciprocity.

- The Board may, without an examination, register as a pharmacist any person who:
- Is registered as a pharmacist in another jurisdiction if the person was required to pass an examination in order to be registered in that jurisdiction.
- Produces evidence satisfactory to the Board that the person has the required secondary and professional education and training and, if a graduate of a foreign school, produces evidence that, before taking the examination for registration in that jurisdiction, the person passed an examination for foreign graduates offered in that jurisdiction which is comparable to the examination required pursuant to paragraph (b) of subsection 1 of NRS 639.120; and
    - Is of good moral character.
    - The provisions of this section apply only if pharmacists registered in this State are granted similar privileges by the state in which the applicant is registered.

NRS 639.136

Expedited certificate by endorsement as registered pharmacist: Requirements; procedure for issuance.

- The Board may issue a certificate by endorsement as a registered pharmacist to an applicant who meets the requirements set forth in this section. An applicant may submit to the Board an application for such a certificate if the applicant holds a corresponding valid and unrestricted certificate as a registered pharmacist in the District of Columbia or any state or territory of the United States.
- An applicant for a certificate by endorsement pursuant to this section must submit to the Board with his or her application: Proof satisfactory to the Board that the applicant: (1)

Satisfies the requirements of subsection 1.

- Has not been disciplined or investigated by the corresponding regulatory authority of the District of Columbia or any state or territory in which the applicant currently holds or has held a certificate as a registered pharmacist; and
- Has not been held civilly or criminally liable for malpractice in the District of Columbia or any state or territory of the United States.
- An affidavit stating that the information contained in the application and any accompanying material is true and correct; and
- Any other information required by the Board.

Not later than 15 business days after receiving an application for a certificate by endorsement as a registered pharmacist pursuant to this section, the Board shall provide written notice to the applicant of any additional information required by the Board to consider the application. Unless the Board denies the application for good cause, the Board shall approve the application and issue a certificate by endorsement as a registered pharmacist to the applicant not later than 45 days after receiving the application. A certificate by endorsement as a registered pharmacist may be issued at a meeting of the Board or between its meetings by the President of the Board. Such an action shall be deemed to be an action of the Board.

NRS 639.1365

Expedited certificate by endorsement as registered pharmacist for active member of Armed Forces, member's spouse, veteran, or veteran's surviving spouse: Requirements; procedure for issuance; provisional certificate pending action on application.

- The Board may issue a certificate by endorsement as a registered pharmacist to an applicant who meets the requirements set forth in this section. An applicant may submit to the Board an application for such a certificate if the applicant:

- Holds a corresponding valid and unrestricted certificate as a registered pharmacist in the District of Columbia or any state or territory of the United States; and
- Is an active member of, or the spouse of an active member of, the Armed Forces of the United States, a veteran or the surviving spouse of a veteran.
- An applicant for a certificate by endorsement pursuant to this section must submit to the Board with his or her application: Proof satisfactory to the Board that the applicant: (1) Satisfies the requirements of subsection 1.
- Has not been disciplined or investigated by the corresponding regulatory authority of the District of Columbia or the state or territory in which the applicant holds a certificate as a registered pharmacist; and
- Has not been held civilly or criminally liable for malpractice in the District of Columbia or any state or territory of the United States.
- An affidavit stating that the information contained in the application and any accompanying material is true and correct; and

Any other information required by the Board.

- Not later than 15 business days after receiving an application for a certificate by endorsement as a registered pharmacist pursuant to this section, the Board shall provide written notice to the applicant of any additional information required by the Board to consider the application. Unless the Board denies the application for good cause, the Board shall approve the application and issue a certificate by endorsement as a registered pharmacist to the applicant not later than 45 days after receiving all the additional information required by the Board to complete the application.

- A certificate by endorsement as a registered pharmacist may be issued at a meeting of the Board or between its meetings by the President of the Board. Such an action shall be deemed to be an action of the Board.
- At any time before making a final decision on an application for a certificate by endorsement pursuant to this section, the Board may grant a provisional certificate as a registered pharmacist to an applicant in accordancewith regulations adopted by the Board.

NRS 639.137

Registration of intern pharmacists: Qualifications; application; issuance of certificate of registration; period of validity of certificate; authorized activities; display; grounds for suspension, termination, or revocation.

- Any person who is not a registered pharmacist, but who is employed in this State for the purpose of fulfilling the requirements of paragraph (d) of subsection 1 of NRS 639.120 to become eligible for registration as a pharmacist, shall register with the Board as an intern pharmacist. An applicant, to be eligible for registration as an intern pharmacist, must be enrolled in a college of pharmacy or a department of pharmacy of a university approved by the Board or be a graduate of a foreign school and pass an examination for foreign graduates approved by the Board. The application must be made on a form furnished by the Board.
- The Executive Secretary of the Board, upon approval of the application, shall issue a certificate of registration authorizing the applicant to undergo practical pharmaceutical training under the direct and immediatesupervision of a registered pharmacist. The period of validity of the certificate of registration, including any renewal, must not exceed 4 years after the date of issue. The certificate of registration authorizes the holder, if acting under the direct and immediate supervision of a registered pharmacist, to perform: The duties of a registered

pharmacist as authorized by regulation of the Board; and(b) Other activities as authorized by regulation of the Board.

- The certificate of registration must be posted as required by NRS 639.150.
- Any certificate of registration issued pursuant to the provisions of this section may be suspended, terminated or revoked by the Board for:
- Any reason set forth in this chapter as grounds for the suspension or revocation of any certificate, licenseor permit; or
- The failure of the registered pharmacist whose name appears on the certificate of registration to provideadequate training and supervision for the intern pharmacist in compliance with regulations adopted by the Board.

NRS 639.1371

Pharmaceutical technicians: Number permitted per pharmacist; qualifications,registration, supervision and authorized services; submission of fingerprints; issuance of provisional registration; regulations.

- The ratio of pharmaceutical technicians to pharmacists must not allow more than one pharmaceutical technician to each pharmacist unless the Board by regulation expands the ratio.
- The Board shall adopt regulations concerning pharmaceutical technicians, including requirements for:(a) The qualifications, registration, and supervision of pharmaceutical technicians; and
- The services which may be performed by pharmaceutical technicians, to ensure the protection and safety of the public in the provision of pharmaceutical care.

- The successful completion of a program for pharmaceutical technicians which is approved by the Board.
- The completion of at least 1,500 hours of experience in carrying out the duties of a pharmaceutical technician; or
- Any other experience or education deemed equivalent by the Board.
- An expanded ratio of pharmaceutical technicians to pharmacists must be appropriate and necessary for aparticular category of pharmacy at any time.
- In addition to the requirements for registration as a pharmaceutical technician adopted by the Board pursuant to subsection 2, each applicant for such registration shall submit with his or her application a completeset of fingerprints and written permission authorizing the Board to forward the fingerprints to the Central Repository for Nevada Records of Criminal History for submission to the Federal Bureau of Investigation for its report. The Board may issue a provisional registration to an applicant pending receipt of the report from the Federal Bureau of Investigation if the Board determines that the applicant is otherwise qualified for registration.

NRS 639.1373

Physician assistant: Authority regarding possession,

administration, prescription and dispensing of controlled substances, poisons, dangerous drugs and devices; registration; regulations.

- A physician assistant licensed pursuant to chapter 630 or 633 of NRS may, if authorized by the Board, possess, administer, prescribe or dispense controlled substances, or possess, administer, prescribe or dispense poisons, dangerous drugs or devices in or out of the presence of his or her supervising physician only to theextent and subject to the limitations specified in the registration certificate issued to the physician assistant by the Board pursuant to this section.

- Each physician assistant licensed pursuant to chapter 630 or 633 of NRS who is authorized by his or her physician assistant's license issued by the Board of Medical Examiners or by the State Board of Osteopathic Medicine, respectively, to possess, administer, prescribe or dispense controlled substances, or to possess, administer, prescribe or dispense poisons, dangerous drugs or devices must apply for and obtain a registration certificate from the Board, pay a fee to be set by regulations adopted by the Board and pass an examination administered by the Board on the law relating to pharmacy before the physician assistant can possess, administer,prescribe or dispense controlled substances, or possess, administer, prescribe or dispense poisons, dangerous drugs or devices.
- The Board shall consider each application separately and may, even though the physician assistant's license issued by the Board of Medical Examiners or by the State Board of Osteopathic Medicine authorizes the physician assistant to possess, administer, prescribe or dispense controlled substances, or to possess, administer, prescribe or dispense poisons, dangerous drugs and devices:

Refuse to issue a registration certificate.

- Issue a registration certificate limiting the authority of the physician assistant to possess, administer, prescribe or dispense controlled substances, or to possess, administer, prescribe or dispense poisons, dangerous drugs or devices, the area in which the physician assistant may possess controlled substances, poisons, dangerous drugs and devices, or the kind and number of controlled substances, poisons, dangerous drugs and devices.
- Issue a registration certificate imposing other limitations or restrictions which the Board feels are

necessary and required to protect the health, safety and welfare of the public.

- The Board shall adopt regulations controlling the maximum amount to be administered, possessed and dispensed, and the storage, security, recordkeeping and transportation of controlled substances and the maximum amount to be administered, possessed, prescribed and dispensed and the storage, security, recordkeeping and transportation of poisons, dangerous drugs and devices by physician assistants licensed.

NRS 639.1375

Advanced practice registered nurses: Authority to dispense controlled substances, poisons, dangerous drugs and devices; registration; regulations.

- Passes an examination administered by the State Board of Nursing on Nevada law relating to pharmacy and submits to the State Board of Pharmacy evidence of passing that examination.
- Is authorized to do so by the State Board of Nursing in a license issued by that Board; and
- Applies for and obtains a certificate of registration from the State Board of Pharmacy and pays the fee setby a regulation adopted by the Board. The Board may set a single fee for the collective certification of advanced practice registered nurses in the employ of a public or nonprofit agency and a different fee for the individual certification of other advanced practice registered nurses.

The State Board of Pharmacy shall consider each application from an advanced practice registered nurse separately, and may:

- Issue a certificate of registration limiting:
- The authority of the advanced practice registered nurse to dispense controlled substances, poisons, dangerous drugs, and devices.

- The area in which the advanced practice registered nurse may dispense.
- The kind and number of controlled substances, poisons, dangerous drugs and devices which the certificate permits the advanced practice registered nurse to dispense; and
- The practice of the advanced practice registered nurse which involves controlled substances, poisons,dangerous drugs and devices in any manner which the Board finds necessary to protect the health, safety and welfare of the public.

- Issue a certificate of registration without any limitation not contained in the license issued by the State Board of Nursing; or
- Refuse to issue a certificate of registration, regardless of the provisions of the license issued by the State Board of Nursing.
- If a certificate of registration issued pursuant to this section is suspended or revoked, the Board may also suspend or revoke the registration of the physician for and with whom the advanced practice registered nurse is inpractice to dispense controlled substances.

  The Board shall adopt regulations setting forth the maximum amounts of any controlled substance, poison, dangerous drug and devices which an advanced practice registered nurse who holds a certificate from the Board may dispense, the conditions under which they must be stored, transported and safeguarded, and the records which each such nurse shall keep.

NRS 639.138

Denial of application: Notice.

- If the Board, after an investigation, denies any application for a certificate, license or permit, the Executive Secretary of the Board shall notify the applicant, within 10 days after the denial is approved by the Board and entered in the official minutes, by registered or certified mail, of thedenial of the application and the reasons therefor. The notice must inform the applicant of the right to petition the Board for reconsideration and the right to submit evidence to controvert the alleged violations on which thedenial was based.

NRS 639.139

Denial of application: Procedure for reconsideration.

- At any time within 30 days after receipt of the notice of denial of an application, the applicant may petition the Board for reconsideration of the application. The petition must set forth a denial, in whole or in part, of the violations alleged and a statement that the applicant is prepared to submit evidence in support of the denial of the allegations.
- Within 30 days after the petition is received by the Board, the Executive Secretary of the Board shall notify the petitioner, by registered or certified mail, of the Board's decision to grant or deny the petition for reconsideration. If the petition is granted, the notice must include the time and place set for reconsideration of theapplication by the Board.

NRS 639.150

Display of certificates, licenses and permits, regulations.

- The holder of a certificate of registration, a license or a permit granted pursuant to the provisions of this chapter shall display the certificate, license or permit, and the current renewal receipt thereof, in the pharmacy conducted by the holder or in which the holder is employed in a place where it may be clearly read by the public.
- A registered pharmacist who is employed or who practices in more than one pharmacy shall post his or her original certificate of registration and the current renewal receipt in the pharmacy in which the pharmacist is primarily employed, in compliance with the provisions of subsection 1, and shall post an 8-inch by 10-inch photocopy of the certificate of registration

and the current renewal receipt in every other pharmacy in which the pharmacist practices on either a part-time or temporary basis.

An institutional pharmacy that serves a majority of inpatients shall display certificates, licenses andpermits in accordance with regulations adopted by the Board.

NRS 639.160

Notice of new place of practice.

- Every registered pharmacist shall, within 10 days after changing his or her place of practice as designated on the books of the Executive Secretary of the Board, notify the Executive Secretary of the change and of the new place of practice. Upon receipt of the notification, the Executive Secretary shall make the necessary change in his or her register.

NRS 639.180

Expiration of certificates, licenses, and permits; procedure for renewal; grounds for refusal to renew; automatic forfeiture for failure to comply with procedure.

- Except as otherwise provided in this subsection, a certificate, license or permit issued by the Board pursuant to this chapter expires on October 31 of each even-numbered year. A certificate of registration as a pharmacist expires on October 31 of each odd-numbered year.
- Each person to whom a certificate, license or permit has been issued may, if the certificate, license or permit has not been revoked, renewthe certificate, license or permit biennially by:

Complying with the requirement of continuing professional education, if applicable.

- If applicable, filing with the Board satisfactory evidence that his or her surety bond or other securityrequired by NRS 639.515 is in full force; an Submitting all information required to complete the renewal.
- The application for renewal, together with the fee for renewal, all required information and

the evidence of compliance with NRS 639.515 must be delivered to the Executive Secretary of the Board on or before the expiration date of the certificate, license or permit, or the current renewal receipt thereof.

- If a certificate, license or permit is renewed, it must be delivered to the applicant within a reasonable time after receipt of the application for renewal and the fee for renewal.
- The Board may refuse to renew a certificate, license or permit if the applicant has committed any act proscribed by NRS 639.210.
- If the application for renewal, the fee for renewal, all required information and the evidence of compliance with NRS 639.515 are not postmarked on or before the expiration date of the certificate, license or permit, or the current renewal receipt thereof, the registration is automatically forfeited.

NRS 639.183

Renewal of registration: Duty of Board to make data request concerning demographic and practice information available to applicants for voluntary completion and electronic submission; confidentiality of information provided.

The Board shall:

- Make the data request developed by the Director of the Department of Health and Human Services pursuant to NRS 439A.116 available to applicants for the renewal of registration as a pharmacist, intern pharmacist, pharmaceutical technician or pharmaceutical technician in training through a link on the electronic application for the renewal of a registration; and
- Request each applicant to complete and electronically submit the data request to the Director.
- The information provided by an applicant for the renewal of a registration pursuant to

subsection 1 is confidential and, except as required by subsection 1, must not be disclosed to any person or entity.

- An applicant for the renewal of a registration is not required to complete a data request pursuant to subsection 1 and is not subject to disciplinary action, including, without limitation, refusal to renew the registration, for failure to do so.

NRS 639.190

Issuance of certificate of registration as pharmacist after forfeiture.

- If a certificate of registration as a pharmacist is forfeited by a person as provided in NRS 639.180, the Board may, within 5 years thereafter, issue a certificate of registration to the person if the Board determines that the person:
- Has not committed any act listed in NRS 639.210 other than the failure to renew the certificate by not submitting the application for renewal or the fee for renewal: and
- Is capable and qualified by education or experience, or both, to practice the profession of pharmacy inthis State.

NRS 639.200

Issuance of duplicate certificates and receipts for renewal.

- The Board shall have thepower to issue duplicate certificates of registration and duplicate renewal receipts upon: Written application therefor signed by the applicant.
- Proof to the satisfaction of the Board that good cause exists for the issuance of the certificate or renewal receipt, and the payment of the proper fees for the issuance thereof.

NRS 639.210

Grounds for suspension or revocation of certificate, license, registration or permit or denial of application.

The Board may suspend or revoke anycertificate, license, registration or permit issued pursuant to this chapter, and deny the application of any person for a certificate, license, registration or permit, if the holder or applicant:

- Is not of good moral character.
- Is guilty of habitual intemperance.
- Becomes or is intoxicated or under the influence of liquor, any depressant drug or a controlled substance,unless taken pursuant to a lawfully issued prescription, while on duty in any establishment licensed by the Board.
- Is guilty of unprofessional
  conduct or conduct contrary to the public interest.
- Has a substance use disorder.
- Has been convicted of a violation of any law or regulation of the Federal Government or of this or any other state related to controlled substances, dangerous drugs, drug samples, or the wholesale or retail distribution of drugs.
- Has been convicted of:
- A felony relating to holding a certificate, license, registration or permit pursuant to
  this chapter.
- Has willfully made to the Board or its authorized representative any false statement which is material to the administration or enforcement of any of the provisions of this chapter.
- Has obtained any certificate, certification, license or permit by the filing of an application, or

any record, affidavit or other information in support thereof, which is false or fraudulent.

- Has violated any provision of the Federal Food, Drug and Cosmetic Act or any other federal law or regulation relating to prescription drugs.
- Has violated, attempted to violate, assisted or abetted in the violation of or conspired to violate any of the provisions of this chapter or any law or regulation relating to drugs, the manufacture or distribution of drugsor the practice of pharmacy, or has knowingly permitted, allowed, condoned or failed to report a violation of any of the provisions of this chapter or any law or regulation relating to drugs, the manufacture or distribution ofdrugs or the practice of pharmacy committed by the holder of a certificate, license, registration or permit;
- Has failed to renew a certificate, license or permit by failing to submit the application for renewal or paythe renewal fee therefor.
- Has had a certificate, license or permit suspended or revoked in another state on grounds which would cause suspension or revocation of a certificate, license or permit in this State.
- Has, as a managing pharmacist, violated any provision of law or regulation concerning recordkeeping orinventory in a store over which he or she presides, or has knowingly allowed a violation of any provision of this chapter or other state or federal laws or regulations relating to the practice of pharmacy by personnel of the pharmacy under his or her supervision.
- Has repeatedly been negligent, which may be evidenced by claims of malpractice settled against him or her.
- Has failed to maintain and make available to a state or federal officer any records in accordance with theprovisions of this chapter.
- An act or omission occurred which resulted in the suspension or revocation of the license pursuant toNRS 449.160.

- This subsection applies to an owner or other principal responsible for the operation of the facility.

NRS 639.210

Grounds for suspension or revocation of certificate, license, registration or permit or denial of application.

The Board may suspend or revoke any certificate, license, registration or permit issued pursuant to this chapter, and deny the application of any person for a certificate, license, registration or permit, if the holder or applicant:

- Becomes or is intoxicated or under the influence of liquor, any depressant drug or a controlled substance, unless taken pursuant to a lawfully issued prescription, while on duty in any establishment licensed by the Board.
- Has been convicted of a violation of any law or regulation of the Federal Government or of this or any other state related to controlled substances, dangerous drugs, drug samples, or the wholesale or retail distribution of drugs.

Has been convicted of:

- A felony relating to holding a certificate, license, registration or permit pursuant to this chapter;(b) A felony pursuant to NRS 639.550 or 639.555; or
- Other crime involving moral turpitude, dishonesty or corruption.
- Has been convicted of violating any of the provisions of NRS 616D.200, 616D.220, 616D.240 or 616D.300 to 616D.440.
- Has willfully made to the Board or its authorized representative any false statement which is material to the administration or enforcement of any of the provisions of this chapter.

- Has obtained any certificate, certification, license or permit by the filing of an application, or any record, affidavit or other information in support thereof, which is false or fraudulent.
- Has violated any provision of the Federal Food, Drug and Cosmetic Act or any other federal law or regulation relating to prescription drugs.
- Has violated, attempted to violate, assisted or abetted in the violation of or conspired to violate any of the provisions of this chapter or any law or regulation relating to drugs, the manufacture or distribution of drugsor the practice of pharmacy, or has knowingly permitted, allowed, condoned or failed to report a violation of any of the provisions of this chapter or any law or regulation relating to drugs, the manufacture or distribution ofdrugs or the practice of pharmacy committed by the holder of a certificate, license, registration or permit.
- Has failed to renew a certificate, license or permit by failing to submit the application for renewal or paythe renewal fee therefor.
- Has had a certificate, license or permit suspended or revoked in another state on grounds which would cause suspension or revocation of a certificate, license or permit in this State.
- Has, as a managing pharmacist, violated any provision of law or regulation concerning recordkeeping orinventory in a store over which he or she presides, or has knowingly allowed a violation of any provision of this chapter or other state or federal laws or regulations relating to the practice of pharmacy by personnel of the pharmacy under his or her supervision.
- Has repeatedly been negligent, which may be evidenced by claims of malpractice settled against him or her.
- Has failed to maintain and make available to a state or federal officer any records in accordance with theprovisions of this chapter or chapter 453 or 454 of NRS;
- Has failed to file or maintain a bond or other security if required by NRS 639.515.

- Has dispensed a self-administered hormonal contraceptive under the protocol established pursuant toNRS 639.28077 without complying with NRS 639.28078; or
- Has operated a medical facility, as defined in NRS 449.0151, at any time during which:(a) The license of the facility was suspended or revoked; or
- An act or omission occurred which resulted in the suspension or revocation of the license pursuant toNRS 449.160.
- This subsection applies to an owner or other principal responsible for the operation of the facility.

NRS 639.211

Mental illness: Immediate suspension of right to practice.

- The adjudication of insanity or mental illness, or the voluntary commitment or admission to any hospital for a mental illness of any certificate holder, shall operate as an immediate suspension of the right of the certificate holder to practice pharmacy in this State, and such suspension shall continue until restoration to or declaration of sanity or mental competence.

NRS 639.212

Mental illness: Reinstatement of suspended certificate, license, registration or permit.

- A person whose certificate, license, registration or permit has been suspended by the Board in accordancewith NRS 639.211 may petition the Board for reinstatement of the certificate, license, registration or permit after restoration or declaration of sanity or mental competence.
- The Board shall not restore any suspended certificate, license, registration or permit until it has found, in a hearing held for that purpose, that with due regard for the public interest the petitioner's right to practice, or to perform the duties and conduct the business covered by the certificate, license, registration or permit, may be safely reinstated.

- In any such hearing the Board may consider the results of its own investigation as well as evidence pertaining to the petitioner's restoration to sanity or mental competence. The affirmative vote of a majority of Board members is necessary to restore the certificate, license, registration or permit. The Board may require, before reinstatement, the petitioner to pass an examination, either oral or written, to determine the petitioner's present fitness to resume his or her practice or conduct his or her business in the public interest.
- In any hearing, conducted for the purpose of reinstating any certificate, license, registration or permit, theBoard may employ expert witnesses considered necessary in order to determine the competency and ability of thepetitioner.
- The Board may grant or deny, without a hearing or argument, any petition for reinstatement filed pursuant to this section, where the petitioner has been afforded a hearing upon any petition filed pursuant to this section within a period of 2 years immediately preceding the filing of the new petition.

NRS 639.2121

Conviction of certain felonies: Immediate suspension of certificate, license, registration or permit; reinstatement.

- The conviction of any person who holds a certificate, license, registration or permit issued pursuant to this chapter of a felony for a violation of any federal law or law of any state concerning drugs or chemicals operates as an immediate suspension of the certificate, license, registration orpermit. The person so convicted may apply to the Board for reinstatement at any time.

NRS 639.2122

Corporations: Denial, suspension and revocation of certificates, licenses, permits or registrations.

- The Board may suspend, revoke or deny any certificate, license, permit or registration of a corporation where conditions exist in relation to any person holding 10 percent or more of the corporate stock of such corporation or to any officer or director of such corporation which would constitute grounds for disciplinary action against such person if he or she were a licensee.

PROFESSIONAL CONDUCT

NRS 639.213

Legislative declaration.

- The Legislature hereby declares the practice of pharmacy to be a learned profession, affecting public safety and welfare and charged with the public interest, and is therefore subject to protection and regulation by the State.

NRS 639.215

Rules.

- The Board may by regulation adopt, amend or repeal rules of professional conduct appropriate to theestablishment and maintenance of a high standard of integrity and dignity in the profession.
- Every registered pharmacist shall be governed by the rules of professional conduct adopted by the Board.3. The rules of professional conduct adopted by the Board shall be furnished to each pharmacist holding a currently valid certificate to practice in this State and to each person to whom a certificate is thereafter issued.

- Upon receipt of a copy of the rules of professional conduct, each registered pharmacist shall subscribe thereto.
- Nothing contained in NRS 639.213, and this section shall be construed as authorizing the Board to adoptrules of professional conduct relating to the issuance of trading stamps to the general public.

CONTINUING PROFESSIONAL EDUCATION

NRS 639.2171

Legislative findings and declaration.

- The Legislature finds and declares that:
- The practice of the profession of pharmacy is directly related to the public health and welfare of the citizens of this State and is subject to regulation and control in the public interest.
- Because of the continuous introduction of new medicinal agents and the changing concepts of the practice of pharmacy, it is essential that a pharmacist undertake a program of continuing education to maintain and improve his or her professional competency.
- To ensure the continued competency of the pharmacist and to maintain uniform qualifications for the licensing of pharmacists to protect the health and welfare of its citizens, the Legislature deems it in the public interest to adopt a program of continuing professional education.

NRS 639.2174

Completion of program prerequisite to renewal of certificate of registered pharmacist.

- The Board shall not renew the certificate of any registered pharmacist until the applicant has submitted proof to the Board of the receipt of the required number of continuing education units, obtainedthrough the satisfactory completion of an accredited program of continuing professional education during the period for which the certificate was issued.

NRS 639.2176

Regulations.

- The Board shall adopt regulations necessary to carry out the purposes of NRS 639.2171 to 639.2176, inclusive, which must include the methods of determining accredited programs, the number of hours of continuing professional education necessary to constitute a continuing education unit, the number of units required of each pharmacist during the period for which a certificate is issued and such other regulations consistent with NRS 639.2171 to 639.2176, inclusive, as the Board may determine to be necessary.

CERTAIN FACILITIES LICENSED BY STATE BOARD OF HEALTH

NRS 639.2177

License; regulations.

The Board shall adopt regulations:

- o As are necessary for the protection of the public appertaining to the safe and efficient acquisition, possession, storage, handling and administration of controlled substances and dangerous drugs in a facility licensed pursuant to this section.

- o To set forth the qualifications, authority and duties of a facility licensed pursuant to this section and the owners, employees and contract employees of the facility.

PHARMACIES

NRS 639.220

Management by registered pharmacist; exceptions; requirements for managingpharmacists; notice of change in managing pharmacist.

- Each pharmacy must be managed by a registered pharmacist, approved by the Board, who is responsible for compliance by the pharmacy and its personnel with all state and federal laws and regulations relating to the operation of the pharmacy and the practice of pharmacy.
- Except as otherwise provided in NRS 639.2321, if the managing pharmacist is the only registered pharmacist employed in the pharmacy, the Board may authorize his or her absence each day for a total period of not to exceed 2 hours for the purpose of taking meals if:
- A registered pharmacist is on call during the absence.
- A sign, as prescribed by regulations of the Board, is posted for public view in the pharmacy indicating theabsence of the pharmacist and the hours of the absence; and
- All drugs, poisons, chemical and restricted devices are kept safe in a manner prescribed by regulations of the Board.
- The authorization required from the Board must be in writing and be retained in the pharmacy and availablefor inspection.
- A person shall not act as a managing pharmacist for more than one licensed pharmacy.
- Each managing pharmacist shall be on duty in the pharmacy and active in the management of the pharmacy full-time, but the managing pharmacist need not be present during the time the pharmacy is open for business if he or she designates another pharmacist employed in the pharmacy to assume the managing pharmacist's duties in his or her absence.

- The managing pharmacist is responsible for the activities of the designee.
- A waiver from the limitation set forth in paragraph (a) may be granted by the Board to the managing pharmacist of a pharmacy located in a hospital with fewer than 100 beds or in a correctional institution housing fewer than 1,500 inmates.
- The Board must be notified before there is a change in the managing pharmacist.

NRS 639.2315

Expedited license by endorsement to conduct pharmacy: Requirements; procedure for issuance.

- The Board may issue a license by endorsement to conduct a pharmacy to an applicant who is a natural person and who meets the requirements set forth in this section. An applicant may submit to the Board an application for such a license if the applicant holds a corresponding valid and unrestricted license to conduct a pharmacy in the District of Columbia or any state or territory of the United States.
- An applicant for a license by endorsement pursuant to this section must submit to the Board with his or her application:
  - Has not been disciplined or investigated by the corresponding regulatory authority of the District of Columbia or any state or territory in which the applicant currently holds or has held a license to conduct a pharmacy; and
  - Has not been held civilly or criminally liable for malpractice in the District of Columbia or any state or territory of the United States.
  - An affidavit stating that the information contained in the application and any accompanying material is true and correct; and any other information required by the Board.

- Not later than 15 business days after receiving an application for a license by endorsement to conduct a pharmacy pursuant to this section, the Board shall provide written notice to the applicant of any additional information required by the Board to consider the application. Unless the Board denies the application for good cause, the Board shall approve the application and issue a license by endorsement to conduct a pharmacy to the applicant not later than 45 days after receiving the application.
- A license by endorsement to conduct a pharmacy may be issued at a meeting of the Board or between its meetings by the President of the Board. Such an action shall be deemed to be an action of the Board.

NRS 639.2316

Expedited license by endorsement to conduct pharmacy for active member of Armed Forces, member's spouse, veteran or veteran's surviving spouse: Requirements; procedure for issuance; provisional license pending action on application.

- The Board may issue a license by endorsement to conduct a pharmacy to an applicant who is a natural person and who meets the requirements set forth in this section. An applicant may submit to the Board an application for such a license if the applicant:
- Holds a corresponding valid and unrestricted license to conduct a pharmacy in the District of Columbia orany state or territory of the United States; and
- Is an active member of, or the spouse of an active member of, the Armed Forces of the United States, a veteran or the surviving spouse of a veteran.
- An applicant for a license by endorsement pursuant to this section must submit to the Board with his or her application:

- Has not been disciplined or investigated by the corresponding regulatory authority of the District of Columbia or the state or territory in which the applicant holds a license to conduct a pharmacy; and
- Has not been held civilly or criminally liable for malpractice in the District of Columbia or any state or territory of the United States.
- An affidavit stating that the information contained in the application and any accompanying material is true and correct; and
- Any other information required by the Board.
- Not later than 15 business days after receiving an application for a license by endorsement to conduct a pharmacy pursuant to this section, the Board shall provide written notice to the applicant of any additional information required by the Board to consider the application. Unless the Board denies the application for good
- cause, the Board shall approve the application and issue a license by endorsement to conduct a pharmacy to the applicant not later than 45 days after receiving all the additional information required by the Board to complete the application.
- A license by endorsement to conduct a pharmacy may be issued at a meeting of the Board or between its meetings by the President of the Board. Such an action shall be deemed to be an action of the Board.
- At any time before making a final decision on an application for a license by endorsement pursuant to this section, the Board may grant a provisional license to conduct a pharmacy to an applicant in accordance with regulations adopted by the Board.

NRS 639.232

Limitations on issuance of licenses.

The Board shall not issue a license to conduct a pharmacy:

- To any practitioner; or
- To any partnership, corporation or association in which a practitioner has a controlling interest or ownsmore than 10 percent of the available stock.

This section does not:

- Apply to a hospital pharmacy or a health maintenance organization which holds a certificate of authorityunder chapter 695C of NRS.
- Prohibit ownership by a practitioner of a building in which a pharmacy is located, if space for thepharmacy is rented at the prevailing rate.

NRS 639.2321

Nuclear pharmacy: Direct supervision of preparation and distribution of radiopharmaceuticals required; qualifications of managing pharmacist; nuclear pharmacist required on premises.

- Any person who prepares or distributes radiopharmaceuticals must be under the direct supervision of a nuclear pharmacist.
- The managing pharmacist of a nuclear pharmacy must be a nuclear pharmacist.
- A nuclear pharmacist must be on the premises during the hours a nuclear pharmacy is open for business.

NRS 639.2322

Nuclear pharmacy: Oral orders; prohibition on refill of prescription for radiopharmaceutical.

- Except as otherwise provided in subsection 2, a managing pharmacist of a nuclear pharmacy may delegate to any person, under the direct supervision of the managing pharmacist, the authority to accept oral orders from a practitioner or the designated agent of a practitioner.
    - An oral order may be used for a radiopharmaceutical which is not prescribed for a specific patient. An oral order which is designated for a specific patient must be accepted only by a nuclear pharmacist or registered intern acting under the direct supervision of a nuclear pharmacist.
    - A prescription for a radiopharmaceutical must not be refilled.
    - As used in this section, "designated agent" means a person who is authorized to communicate a practitioner's instructions to a nuclear pharmacy.

NRS 639.2324

Institutional pharmacies: Requirements for operation.

The operation of an institutional pharmacy must meet the following requirements:

- In a hospital with 100 or more beds, the pharmacy must be under the continuous supervision of a pharmacist during the time it is open for pharmaceutical services.
- In a hospital with less than 100 beds, the services of a pharmacist may be on less than a full-time basis, depending upon the needs of the institution, and pursuant to the regulations and recommendations of the State Board of Pharmacy and the person charged with the administration and control of the institution.
- In the absence of a pharmacist from the pharmacy, a nurse or practitioner designated by the pharmacist may obtain from the pharmacy such necessary

quantities of drugs to administer to a patient until the pharmacy reopens as are ordered by a medical practitioner and needed by a patient in an emergency. The pharmacist in charge of the institutional pharmacy shall initiate procedures to provide foradministration and technical guidance in all matters pertaining to the acquiring, stocking, recordkeeping and dispensing of drugs and devices.

NRS 639.2326

Pharmacies in correctional institutions: Supervision by prescribing practitioner or licensed pharmacy; security; records.

- Except as otherwise provided in NRS 639.2327, a pharmacy in a correctional institution which is usedmainly for storage, and from which controlled substances and dangerous drugs and devices are administered must be supervised by a prescribing practitioner or a licensed pharmacy.
- The practitioner or a registered pharmacist need not be present at the times the pharmacy is open but is responsible for the security of the pharmacy and shall maintain the records required by the Board. In any case, thename of the prescribing practitioner must be recorded when any controlled substance, dangerous drug or device isadministered or ordered for stock.

NRS 639.2327

Maintenance of stocks of drugs by certain facilities.

- A facility for intermediate care or facility for skilled nursing which is licensed as such by the Division of Public and Behavioral Health of the Department of Health and Human Services and is registered with the Board pursuant to this chapter may maintaina stock of drugs for

- emergency treatment of inpatients, subject to the following conditions:
- The Board shall by regulation determine the specific drugs and the quantities thereof which may be maintained.
- The emergency stock of drugs must be maintained at all times in a solid, sealed container and the seal must remain intact except when the drugs are needed for emergency treatment of a patient in the facility. The sealed container must be stored at all times in a locked compartment on the premises of the facility.
- All drugs delivered to a facility must be signed for by the nurse or other person in charge. An inventory
- of the stock of drugs must be appended to the sealed container. Immediately after the drugs are needed, the physician or registered nurse who breaks the seal shall enter on the inventory sheet the following information:
- The date and time the sealed container is opened;
- The name of the patient for whom the drugs are to be used.
- The name of the patient's physician or the physician who directs the administration of the drugs, if different.
- An itemization of the drugs removed; and
- The signature of the person who opened the sealed container.
- When the drugs have been removed and the information required by subsection 3 has been entered on the inventory, the physician or registered nurse shall immediately replace the container in a locked compartment and shall notify the pharmaceutical consultant, as soon as it is practical to do so, that the container has been opened.
- The sealed container and its contents at all times remain the responsibility of the

pharmaceutical

- consultant. Upon being notified that the sealed container has been opened, or on the next business day if notification is not received during business hours, but in no event more than 48 hours following receipt of the notification, the pharmaceutical consultant shall:

NRS 639.23275

Delivery of controlled substance or dangerous drug to hospital, recovery center, facility for intermediate care or facility for skilled nursing which does not have pharmacy on premises.

- Except as otherwise provided in NRS 453.256, no pharmacy may deliver a controlled substance or dangerous drug for a specific patient to a hospital, recovery center, facility for intermediate care or facility for skilled nursing which is licensed as such by the Division of Public and Behavioral Health of the Department of Health and Human Services which does not have a pharmacy on the premises except pursuant to a prescription given:
- Directly from the prescribing practitioner to a pharmacist.
- If an order for entry on a chart is given by a prescribing practitioner, the chart order must be signed by thepractitioner who authorized the administration of the drug within 48 hours after the order is given by that practitioner.

NRS 639.23277

Remote sites and satellite consultation sites: Location; operation; regulations.

In addition to the requirements set forth in this chapter and any other specific statute, a remote site orsatellite consultation site must be located:

- At least 50 miles or more from the nearest pharmacy; and
- A pharmaceutical technician without the physical presence of a managing pharmacist, except

that the managing pharmacist of the telepharmacy shall also be deemed the managing pharmacist of the remote site or satellite consultation site; or

- A dispensing technician without the physical presence of a dispensing practitioner, except that the dispensing practitioner of the telepharmacy shall also be deemed the managing pharmacist of the remote site or satellite consultation site.
- The Board shall adopt regulations for the purposes of this section, which establish the manner of determining a "service area." Such a "service area" must be a geographical area of between 5 and 10 miles in radius. In adopting the regulations, the Board may consider, without limitation, the ease or difficulty of access to the nearest pharmacy and the availability of roadways.

NRS 639.2328

Pharmacy located outside Nevada: Licensing; requirements; notice of licensing of Canadian pharmacy; recommendation that licensed Canadian pharmacy be included on website.

- Every pharmacy located outside Nevada that provides mail order service to or solicits or advertises fororders for drugs available with a prescription from a resident of Nevada must be licensed by the Board.
- To be licensed or to renew a license, such a pharmacy must:
- Be licensed as a pharmacy, or the equivalent, by the state or country in which its dispensing facilities arelocated.
- Pay the fee required by regulation of the Board.
- Submit evidence satisfactory to the Board that the facility, records and operation of the pharmacy comply with the laws and regulations of the state or country in which the pharmacy is located.

- Submit certification satisfactory to the Board that the pharmacy complies with all lawful requests and directions from the regulatory board or licensing authority of the state or country in which the pharmacy islocated relating to the shipment, mailing or delivery of drugs.

NRS 639.23282

Pharmacy located outside Nevada: Considerations required by Board before issuing license.

- Before issuing a license to a pharmacy located outside Nevada that provides mail order service to a resident of Nevada, the Board shall consider:
- The qualifications and credentials of the applicant; and

  Any suspension or revocation of a license or restriction on a license held by the applicant.

NRS 639.23286

Pharmacy located outside Nevada: Substitution of drug; toll-free telephone service.

- A pharmacy located outside Nevada that provides mail order service to a resident of Nevada:
- May substitute a drug if the substitution is made in accordance with the provisions of the laws and regulations of the state or country in which the pharmacy is located.
- Shall provide a toll-free telephone service for its customers to a pharmacist who has access to the recordsof the customers from Nevada. The telephone service must be available for not less than 5 days per week and for at least 40 hours per week. The telephone number must be disclosed on the label attached to each container of drugs dispensed to a resident of Nevada.

NRS 639.23288

Internet pharmacy: Certification required; regulations; Board required to post onInternet site list of certified Internet pharmacies and related information.

- In addition to the requirements set forth in this chapter and any other specific statute, an Internetpharmacy located:
- Within this State, shall not fill or refill a prescription or otherwise engage in the practice of pharmacy fora person located within or outside this State unless the Internet pharmacy is certified by the Board.
- Outside this State, shall not fill or refill a prescription or otherwise engage in the practice of pharmacy fora person located within this State unless the Internet pharmacy is certified by the Board.
- The Board shall adopt regulations prescribing standards for certifying an Internet pharmacy. The standards adopted by the Board may be based upon standards adopted by the National Association of Boards of Pharmacy or some other association or organization that provides standards for certifying an Internet pharmacy.
- The Board shall post on a website or other Internet site that is operated or administered by or on behalf ofthe Board:

A list of Internet pharmacies certified by the Board; and

NRS 639.233

License required.

- Any person, including a wholesaler or manufacturer, who engages in the business of wholesale distribution or furnishing controlled substances, poisons, drugs, devices or appliances that are restricted byfederal law to sale by or on the order of a physician to any person located within this State shall obtain a license pursuant to the provisions of this chapter.

NRS 639.2345

Sale of veterinary drugs: Permit required; regulations; exemption.

- Any person who engages in the sale of veterinary prescription or nonprescription drugs must obtain a permit from the Board. The Board shall adopt regulations specifying the fee for the permit, requirements for the refrigeration and storage of drugs and other matters relating to the permit.

NRS 639.235

Persons authorized to prescribe and write prescriptions; procedure for filling certain prescriptions written by persons not licensed in this State.

- No person other than a practitioner holding a license to practice his or her profession in this State may prescribe or write a prescription, except that a prescription written by a person who is not licensed to practice in this State, but is authorized by the laws of another state to prescribe, shall be deemed to be a legal prescription unless the person prescribed or wrote the prescription in violation of the provisions of NRS 453.3611 to 453.3648, inclusive.
- If a prescription that is prescribed by a person who is not licensed to practice in this State, but is authorized by the laws of another state to prescribe, calls for a controlled substance listed in:
- Schedule II, the registered pharmacist who is to fill the prescription shall establish and document that the prescription is authentic and that a bona fide relationship between the patient and the person prescribing the controlled substance did exist when the prescription was written.

Schedule III or IV, the registered pharmacist who is to fill the prescription shall establish that the prescription is authentic and that a bona fide relationship between the patient and the person prescribing the controlled substance did exist when the prescription was written. This paragraph does not require the registered pharmacist to inquire into such a relationship upon the receipt of a similar prescription subsequently issued for that patient.

- A pharmacist who fills a prescription described in subsection 2 shall record on the prescription or in the prescription record in the pharmacy's computer:
- The date and time the patient was examined by the person prescribing the controlled substance for which the prescription was issued.
- For the purposes of subsection 2, a bona fide relationship between the patient and the person prescribing the controlled substance shall be deemed to exist if the patient was examined in person, electronically, telephonically or by fiber optics, including, without limitation, through telehealth, within or outside this State or the United States by the person prescribing the controlled substances within the 6 months immediately preceding the date the prescription was issued.

NRS 639.2351

Advanced practice registered nurse: Authority to prescribe controlled substances, poisons, dangerous drugs and devices; registration.

- An advanced practice registered nurse may prescribe, in accordance with NRS 454.695 and 632.237,controlled substances, poisons, dangerous drugs and devices if the advanced practice registered nurse:
- Is authorized to do so by the State Board of Nursing in a license issued by that Board; and
- Applies for and obtains a certificate of registration from the State Board of Pharmacy and

pays the fee setby a regulation adopted by the Board.

- The State Board of Pharmacy shall consider each application from an advanced practice registered nurseseparately, and may:
- Issue a certificate of registration; or
- Refuse to issue a certificate of registration, regardless of the provisions of the license issued by the StateBoard of Nursing.

NRS 639.2352

Inclusion of information regarding symptom or purpose of prescription on label attached to container; practitioners required to post notice.

- Before issuing a prescription, a practitioner may ask the patient whether he or she wishes to have included on the label attached to the container of the drug the symptom or purpose for which the drug is prescribed. If the patient requests that the information be included on the label, the practitioner shall include on the prescription the symptom or purpose for which the drug is prescribed.
- Each practitioner shall post in a conspicuous location in each room used for the examination of a patienta sign which is not less than 8.5 inches wide and not less than 11 inches high and which contains, in at least 12- point boldface type, the following:

NOTICE TO PATIENTS

- You have the right to have the symptom or purpose for which a drug is prescribed included on the labelattached to the container of your prescribed drug.
- You have the right to ask the person writing your prescription to instruct the pharmacy to print thisinformation on the label attached to the container of your prescribed drug.
- Having the purpose or symptom printed on the label attached to the container of your

drug may help youto properly use and track your prescribed drugs.

NRS 639.2355

Practitioner liable for prescription orally transmitted by agent.

- A practitioner is liablefor any order for a prescription which his or her agent orally transmits to a pharmacist.

NRS 639.236

Numbering, filing and retention of prescriptions; inspection of files; regulations.

- All prescriptions filled by a practitioner must be serially numbered and filed in the manner prescribed by regulation of the Board. Prescriptions for controlled substances listed in schedule II must be filed separately fromother prescriptions or in a readily retrievable manner as the Board may provide by regulation. All prescriptions must be retained on file for at least 2 years.
- Each prescription on file must bear the date on which it was originally filled and be personally signed or
- initialed by the registered pharmacist or practitioner who filled it.
- Files of prescriptions are open to inspection by members, inspectors and investigators of the Board and by inspectors of the Food and Drug Administration and agents of the Investigation Division of the Department of Public Safety.

NRS 639.238

Prescriptions not public records: pharmacists not to divulge contents; exceptions; procedure for providing copy of prescription to authorized persons and other pharmacists.

- Prescriptions filled and on file in a pharmacy are not a public record. Except as otherwise provided in NRS 439.538 and 639.2357, a pharmacist shall not divulge the contents of any prescription or provide a copy of any prescription, except to:
- The patient for whom the original prescription was issued.
- A member, inspector or investigator of the Board or an inspector of the Food and Drug Administration oran agent of the Investigation Division of the Department of Public Safety.
- An agency of state government charged with the responsibility of providing medical care for the patient; (f) An insurance carrier, on receipt of written authorization signed by the patient or his or her legal guardian, authorizing the release of such information.
- Any person authorized by an order of a district court.
- Any member, inspector or investigator of a professional licensing board which licenses a practitioner whoorders prescriptions filled at the pharmacy.
- Other registered pharmacists for the limited purpose of and to the extent necessary for the exchange ofinformation relating to persons who are suspected of:
    - Misusing prescriptions to obtain excessive amounts of drugs; or
    - Failing to use a drug in conformity with the directions for its use or taking a drug in combinationwith other drugs in a manner that could result in injury to that person.

NRS 639.23914

Prescription medication agreement required for prescriptions for certain controlled substances issued for more than 30 days: contents.

- If a practitioner, other than a veterinarian, intends to prescribe a controlled substance listed in schedule II,III or IV for more than 30 days for the treatment of pain, the practitioner must, not later than 30 days after issuingthe initial prescription, enter into a prescription medication agreement with the patient, which must be:
- Documented in the record of the patient; and
- Updated at least once every 365 days while the patient is using the controlled substance or whenever a change is made to the treatment plan established pursuant to paragraph (c) of subsection 1 of NRS 639.23911.
- A prescription medication agreement entered into pursuant to subsection 1 must include, without limitation:
- The goals of the treatment of the patient.
- Consent of the patient to testing to monitor drug use when deemed medically necessary by the practitioner.
- A requirement that the patient take the controlled substance only as prescribed;(d) A prohibition on sharing medication with any other person.

NRS 639.2392

Controlled substance or dangerous drug: Records.

- A record of each refill of any prescription for a controlled substance or dangerous drug or anyauthorization to refill such a prescription must be kept:

NRS 639.2393

Controlled substance or dangerous drug: Limitations.

- Any prescription for a controlled substance, regardless of the authorization to refill given by the prescribing practitioner, must not be refilled more than five times or after 6 months have elapsed from the date it was originally issued and may be refilled only in keeping with the number of doses ordered and the directions for use.
- Any prescription for a dangerous drug, regardless of the authorization to refill given by the prescribing practitioner, must not be refilled after 1 year has elapsed from the date it was originally issued and may be refilledonly in keeping with the number of doses ordered and the directions for use.
- If no authorization to refill is given by the prescribing practitioner, or if the prescription is refillable and
- has been refilled for the number of times or for the period set forth in subsection 1 or 2, the original prescriptionis invalid and a new prescription must be obtained and placed in the prescription file.

NRS 639.2394

Controlled substance or dangerous drug: Exercise of judgment by pharmacist.

- In theabsence of specific authorization to refill, when the refilling of a prescription calling for a controlled substance ordangerous drug needed for the continuation of a treatment of a chronic or continuing illness is considered necessary and the pharmacist is unable to communicate with the prescribing practitioner, the pharmacist may, if in his or her professional judgment the pharmacist feels that the controlled substance or dangerous drug should beprovided for the patient, furnish a sufficient supply of the medication to provide for the continuation of treatment until such time as he or she can communicate with the prescribing practitioner personally.

NRS 639.2395

Early refills for topical ophthalmic products authorized under certain circumstances.

- Except as otherwise provided in subsection 2, a pharmacist, upon the request of a patient having difficulty with inadvertent wastage of a topical ophthalmic product, and pursuant to a valid prescription which bears specific authorization to refill, shall dispense a refill of the product:
- After 21 days or more but before 30 days after the patient has received any 30-day supply of the product.
- After 42 days or more but before 60 days after the patient has received any 60-day supply of the product.
- After 63 days or more but before 90 days after the patient has received any 90-day supply of the product.2. The provisions of subsection 1 do not:

NRS 639.2396

Specific authorization; limitations.

- Except as otherwise provided by subsection 2 and NRS 639.23965, a prescription which bears specific authorization to refill, given by the prescribing practitioner at the time he or she issued the original prescription,or a prescription which bears authorization permitting the pharmacist to refill the prescription as needed by the patient, may be refilled for the number of times authorized or for the period authorized if it was refilled in accordance with the number of doses ordered and the directions for use.
- Except as otherwise provided in NRS 639.28075, a pharmacist may, in his or her professional

judgment and pursuant to a valid prescription that specifies an initial amount of less than a 90-day supply of a drug other than a controlled substance followed by periodic refills of the initial amount of the drug, dispense not more than a90-day supply of the drug if:

- The patient has used an initial 30-day supply of the drug, or the drug has previously been prescribed to the patient in a 90-day supply.
- The total number of dosage units that are dispensed pursuant to the prescription does not exceed the total number of dosage units, including refills, that are authorized on the prescription by the prescribing practitioner; and
- The prescribing practitioner has not specified on the prescription that dispensing the prescription in an initial amount of less than a 90-day supply followed by periodic refills of the initial amount of the drug is medically necessary.

NRS 639.2597

Use of list of biologically equivalent drugs or interchangeable biological products.

- A pharmacist or practitioner who proposes to make any substitution must have made use of a list of biologically equivalent drugs or interchangeable biological products approved by the United States Food and Drug Administration.

Collaborative Practice of Pharmacy; Collaborative Drug Therapy Management

NRS 639.2623

Authority: requirements to enter into collaborative practice agreement; duties of pharmacist; patient consent required; conditions and limitations.

- A pharmacist who has entered into a valid collaborative practice agreement may engage in the collaborative practice of pharmacy or collaborative drug therapy management at any location in this State.

- To enter into a collaborative practice agreement, a practitioner must:
- Be licensed in good standing to practice his or her profession in this State; and
- Agree to obtain the informed, written consent from a patient who is referred by the practitioner to a pharmacist pursuant to a collaborative practice agreement for collaborative drug therapy management. Theprovisions of this paragraph must not be construed to require a patient to obtain a referral from a practitioner before a pharmacist may engage in the collaborative practice of pharmacy or collaborative drug therapy management.
- A practitioner shall not enter into a collaborative practice agreement with a collaborating pharmacist if the geographic distance between the practitioner and the collaborating pharmacist prevents or limits effective collaboration in the delivery of care or treatment to patients.
- Except as otherwise provided in this subsection, a practitioner shall not enter a collaborative practice agreement that includes diagnosis or initiating treatment unless the practitioner actively practices his or her profession in this State or provides those services using telehealth. The Board may grant a written request for an exemption from the requirements of this subsection for good cause shown.
- A collaborative practice agreement must not grant a pharmacist the authority to engage in an activity thatis outside the scope of the current practice of the practitioner.
- A pharmacist who engages in the collaborative practice of pharmacy shall:
- Except as otherwise provided in paragraph (b), document any treatment or care provided to a patient pursuant to a collaborative practice agreement after providing such treatment or care in the medical record of the patient, on the chart of the patient or in a separate logbook.

- Document in the medical record of the patient, on the chart of the patient or in a separate logbook any decision or action concerning the management of drug therapy pursuant to a collaborative practice agreement after making such a decision or taking such an action;
- Maintain all records concerning the care or treatment provided to a patient pursuant to a collaborative practice agreement in written or electronic form for at least 7 years.
- Comply with all provisions of the Health Insurance Portability and Accountability Act of 1996, Public Law 104-191, the regulations adopted pursuant thereto, and all other federal and state laws and regulations concerning the privacy of information regarding health care; and
- Provide a patient with written notification of:
- Any test administered by the pharmacist and the results of such a test.
- The name of any drug or prescription filled and dispensed by the pharmacist to the patient; and(3) The contact information of the pharmacist.
- A pharmacist shall obtain the informed, written consent of a patient before engaging in the collaborative practice of pharmacy on behalf of the patient. Such written consent must include, without limitation, a statement that the pharmacist:
- May initiate, modify or discontinue the medication of the patient pursuant to a collaborative practice agreement; and
- Is not a physician, osteopathic physician, advanced practice registered nurse or physician assistant?
- A pharmacy must not require a registered pharmacist, as a condition of employment, to enter into a collaborative practice agreement.

NRS 639.2627

Requirements for contents of and submission of collaborative practice agreement; expiration and renewal of agreement.

- A collaborative practice agreement must be signed by each practitioner and pharmacist who enter into the agreement and submitted to the Board in written and electronic form. A collaborative practice agreement must include:
- A description of the types of decisions concerning the management of drug therapy that the pharmacist is authorized to make, which may include a specific description of the diseases and drugs for which the pharmacist is authorized to manage drug therapy.
- A detailed explanation of the procedures that the pharmacist must follow when engaging in the collaborative practice of pharmacy, including, without limitation, the manner in which the pharmacist must document decisions concerning treatment and care in accordance with subsection 6 of NRS 639.2623, report such decisions to the practitioner and receive feedback from the practitioner.
- The procedure by which the pharmacist will notify the practitioner of an adverse event concerning the
- health of the patient.
- The procedure by which the practitioner will provide the pharmacist with a diagnosis of the patient and any other medical information necessary to carry out the patient's drug therapy management.
- A description of the means by which the practitioner will monitor clinical outcomes of a patient and intercede when necessary to protect the health of the patient or accomplish the goals of the treatment prescribed for the patient.

- Authorization for the practitioner to override the agreement if necessary to protect the health of the patientor accomplish the goals of the treatment prescribed for the patient.
- Authorization for either party to terminate the agreement by written notice to the other party, which must include, without limitation, written notice to the patient that informs the patient of the procedures by which he or she may continue drug therapy.
- The effective date of the agreement.
- The date by which a review must be conducted pursuant to subsection 2 for the renewal of the agreement, which must not be later than the expiration date of the agreement.
- The address of the location where the records described in subsection 6 of NRS 639.2623 will be maintained; and
- The process by which the pharmacist will obtain the informed, written consent required by subsection 7 of NRS 639.2623.
- A collaborative practice agreement must expire not later than 1 year after the date on which the agreement becomes effective. The parties to a collaborative practice agreement may renew the agreement after reviewing the agreement and making any necessary revisions.

NRS 639.263

False or misleading advertising.

No registered pharmacist or owner of any pharmacy licensed under the provisions of this chapter may make, disseminate or cause to be made or disseminated before the public in this state, in any newspaper or other publication, or any advertising device, or in any other manneror means whatever, any statement concerning prices or services, professional or otherwise, which is untrue or misleading, and which is known, or which by the exercise of reasonable care should be known, to be false or misleading.

NRS 639.264

Prohibition against unearned rebate, refund or other consideration for referrals.

- No registered pharmacist, or owner of any pharmacy licensed under the provisions of this chapter, may offer, deliver or pay any unearned rebate, refund, commission, preference, patronage dividend, discount or other unearned consideration to any person, whether in the form of money or otherwise, as compensation or inducement to such person for referring prescriptions, patients, clients or customers to such pharmacist orpharmacy, irrespective of any membership, proprietary interest or co-ownership in or with any person by whom such prescriptions, patients, clients or customers are referred.
- The furnishing to a practitioner by a pharmacist or a pharmacy of prescription blanks bearing the name or name and address of any pharmacy is an unearned rebate and an inducement to refer patients to such pharmacist or pharmacy.

NRS 639.265

Pharmacists may trade or exchange drugs if necessary for business.

- A registered pharmacist may trade or exchange drugs with another such pharmacist when any such trade or exchange is necessary to the business of such pharmacist.

PRODUCTS THAT ARE PRECURSORS TO METHAMPHETAMINE

NRS 639.400

"Product that is a precursor to methamphetamine" defined.

- As used in NRS 639.400 to 639.450, inclusive, "product that is a precursor to methamphetamine" means a product which contains ephedrine, pseudoephedrine or phenylpropanolamine or the salts, optical isomers or salts of optical isomers of such chemicals and may be marketed or distributed lawfully in the United States under the Federal Food,

Drug and Cosmetic Act, 21 U.S.C. §§ 301 et seq., as a nonprescription drug.

NRS 639.410

Sales of products that are precursors to methamphetamine.

- A person shall not sell or transfer to an ultimate user in the course of any business or engage in the business of selling to ultimate users, a product that is a precursor to methamphetamine, unless the person is a pharmacy.

NRS 639.420

Report of unusual or excessive loss or disappearance of products that are precursors to methamphetamine by pharmacy: Requirement; exception; contents.

- Except as otherwise provided in subsection 2, if a pharmacy becomes aware of any unusual or excessive loss or disappearance of a product that is a precursor to methamphetamine while the product is under the control of the pharmacy, the pharmacy must:
- Make an oral report to the Department of Public Safety at the earliest practicable opportunity after the pharmacy becomes aware of the unusual or excessive loss or disappearance of the product that is a precursor to methamphetamine; and Submit a written report to the Department of Public Safety within 15 days after the pharmacy becomes aware of the unusual or excessive loss or disappearance of the product that is a precursor to methamphetamine.
- If an unusual or excessive loss or disappearance of a product that is a precursor to methamphetamine occurs while the product is being transported to a pharmacy, the pharmacy is not required to comply with the provisions of subsection 1.
- A report required by subsection 1 must include, without limitation, a description of the circumstances surrounding the loss or disappearance and may be in substantially the following form:

- As used in this section, "unusual or excessive loss or disappearance" means a loss or disappearance for which a report would be required under 21 U.S.C. § 830(b)(1), and any regulations adopted pursuant thereto, if the pharmacy were subject to the requirements of 21 U.S.C. § 830(b)(1) and any regulations adopted pursuant thereto.

NRS 639.430

Real-time, stop sale system: Conditions for approval; regulations.

- The Board shall approve a real-time, stop sale system for use by pharmacies in this State if the Board determines that a real-time, stop sale system is available and appropriate for use by pharmacies in this State. The Board shall approve a real-time, stop sale system for use by pharmacies in this State only if the Board determines that the system:
- Will allow pharmacies in this State to electronically submit information to the system before the sale or transfer of a product that is a precursor to methamphetamine.
- Will determine whether the sale or transfer of the product would violate NRS 453.355 or any other law which prohibits the sale or transfer of a product that is a precursor to methamphetamine;
- Will send an alert to pharmacies to stop the sale or transfer of a product if the sale or transfer would violate NRS 453.355 or any other law which prohibits the sale or transfer of a product that is a precursor to methamphetamine;
- Will allow law enforcement agencies in this State to access from the system transaction records of any sale or transfer or attempted sale or transfer of a product that is a precursor to methamphetamine; and
- Is available for use by pharmacies and law enforcement agencies in this State free of charge.
- Before approving a real-time, stop sale system, the Board must adopt regulations establishing

the minimum requirements for the real-time, stop sale system. The Board shall also adopt regulations establishing the requirements for use of the real-time, stop sale system by the pharmacies and law enforcement agencies of this State.

NRS 639.440

Real-time, stop sale system: Notification of pharmacies; duties of pharmacy; civil immunity; penalty.

- After the Board has approved a real-time, stop sale system pursuant to NRS 639.430 and adopted regulations establishing the requirements for the use of the system pursuant to that section, the Board must notify each pharmacy in this State of the real-time, stop sale system that has been approved, the manner in which to establish the system in the pharmacy and the content of the regulations.
- Once a pharmacy receives notification pursuant to subsection 1, the pharmacy shall obtain the real-time, stop sale system and consult the system in the manner prescribed before completing any sale or transfer of a product that is a precursor to methamphetamine, except when the purchaser has a valid prescription for such a product. The pharmacy shall obtain any information necessary from the person seeking the purchase or transfer of the product to receive notice from the real-time, stop sale system.
- Except as otherwise provided in this subsection, if a pharmacy receives an alert from the real-time, stop sale system that the sale or transfer of a product may violate NRS 453.355 or any other law which prohibits the sale or transfer of a product that is a precursor to methamphetamine, the pharmacy must not allow the sale or transfer to be completed. The Board shall provide by regulation for exceptions to allow for the completion of a sale or transfer:

- Despite such an alert if the pharmacist or an employee of the pharmacy has a reasonable fear of imminentbodily harm.
- If a pharmacy experiences a mechanical or electronic failure of the real-time, stop sale system.
- A pharmacy that complies with the provisions of this section is not liable in any civil action for using the real-time, stop sale system or for any act or omission resulting from the use of the system which is not the result of the negligence, recklessness or deliberate misconduct of the pharmacy.
- Failure of a person to use the real-time, stop sale system as required pursuant to this section is a misdemeanor punishable by a fine of not more than $1,000.

NRS 639.450

Real-time, stop sale system: Immunity of Board from liability for unauthorized access or misuse of information collected by or derived from system.

- The failure of the real-time, stop sale system
- approved pursuant to NRS 639.430 to send an alert to a pharmacy to stop the sale or transfer of a product that is aprecursor to methamphetamine in violation of NRS 453.355, or any other law which prohibits the sale or transfer of a product that is a precursor to methamphetamine, does not establish a basis for any cause of action against theBoard. The Board is immune from any liability arising from or related to the unauthorized access or misuse ofany information collected by or derived from the real-time, stop sale system approved pursuant to NRS 639.430.

PART TWO

NEVADA PHARMACY LAW QUESTIONS

1. A Pharmacist may dispense a product containing pseudoephedrine without a prescription to a person who is at least __________ years old.

    b. 14 years

    c. 16 years

    d. 18 years

    e. No age limits

2. How many hours of practical experience is required by the Nevada board?

    a. 1000 hours

    b. 1250 hours

    c. 1450 hours

    d. 1740 hours

3. Pharmacy technician is required to complete at least ___________ hours of training and experience to qualify.

    a. 1000 hours

    b. 1200 hours

    c. 1500 hours

    d. 1600 hours

4. Schedule II controlled prescriptions for patients in a LTCF or patients with a medical diagnosis documenting a terminal illness are valid for a period not to exceed____________ from the issue date.

    a. 30 days
    b. 60 days
    c. 90 days
    d. 120 days

5. The remaining portion of schedule II prescription may be filled within__________ hours after the first partial filling.

    a. 24 hours
    b. 36 hours
    c. 48 hours
    d. 72 hours

6. A facsimile prescription of schedule III drug received by the pharmacy must be kept by the pharmacist for at least____________ years after it is received by him.

    a. 1 year
    b. 2 years
    c. 3 years
    d. 4 years

7. In Nevada, the inventory of controlled substances should be done every:

    a. 1 year
    b. 2 years
    c. 3 years
    d. 4 years

8. In Nevada, inventory records must be maintained for a period of at least:

   a. 1 year

   b. 2 years

   c. 3 years

   d. 4 years

9. In Nevada, a pharmacist is required to collect ____________CE hours every renewal period.

   a. 10 hours

   b. 20 hours

   c. 30 hours

   d. 40 hours

10. An emergency oral prescription for Schedule II controlled drugs must be mailed to dispensing pharmacy by an authorized prescriber within:

    a. 48 hours after an oral authorization.

    b. 7 days after an oral authorization.

    c. 10 days after an oral authorization.

    d. 72 hours after an oral authorization.

11. Who may appoint the members of the Nevada State Pharmacy Board?

    a. Director of Pharmacy Board

    b. Governor

    c. Drug inspector of the state

    d. Healthcare administers of the state

12. How many days must a C-2 prescription be received by the pharmacy after it is issued.

    a. 14 days.
    b. 30 days.
    c. 60 days.
    d. 90 days

13. What is the latest do not fill date a prescriber may write on a prescription?

    a. 3 months.
    b. 90 days.
    c. 6 months.
    d. 9 months

14. What is the longest day's supply that can be dispensed using a post-dated prescription?

    a. 30 days.
    b. 60 days.
    c. 90 days.
    d. 120 days

15. What is the maximum morphine milligram equivalents (MME) that may be dispensed to a opioid-naive patient receiving an initial prescription for acute pain?

    a. 60.
    b. 90.
    c. 100.
    d. 120.

16. How many Pharmaceutical Technicians are allowed for each pharmacist on duty?

   a. 2 technicians.

   b. 3 technicians.

   c. 4 technicians.

   d. 5 technicians

17. A pharmacist receives a prescription for 40 Percocet tablets, but the pharmacy has only 15 tablets in stock. The patient accepts the 15 tablets. How much time does the pharmacist have to provide the remaining 25 tablets?

   a. 24 hours

   b. 72 hours

   c. 96 hours

   d. 6 months

18.. Which of the following is a correct DEA number for a Dr. Andrea J. Shedlock, who was Dr. Andrea Costello when she requested her DEA number before she was married?

   a. AC1234563

   b. AS1234563

   c. JC1234563

   d. JS1234563

19. What form is used to report the theft of con- trolled substances?

a. DEA Form 41

b. DEA Form 106

c. DEA Form 222

d. DEA Form 224

20. What classification of drug recall will cause serious adverse health consequences or death?

a. Class I

b. Class II

c. Class III

d. Class IV

21. Which of the following addresses nonsterile compounding?

a. ISO 9000

b. USP 790.

c. USP 795.

d. USP 797.

22. What is the maximum amount of pseudoephedrine base that may be purchased in 1 day?

   a. 2.4 g

   b. 3.6 g

   c. 9 g

   d. 10 g

23. How long is a pharmacy's DEA permit valid?

   a. 1 year

   b. 2 years

   c. 3 years

   d. 4 years

24. What is DEA form 222 used for?

   a. To report the theft of controlled substances.

   b. To document the destruction of controlled substances.

   c. To order Schedule II medications.

   d. To prescribe Schedule II medications.

25. The Red Book is a resource that focuses on:

   a. Therapeutic equivalence evaluations.

   b. Labeled and unlabeled uses of medications.

   c. Pharmacokinetics.

   d. Drug pricing.

26. If a drug has no accepted medical use and extremely high potential for abuse, which DEA schedule would it be categorized in?

    a. Schedule I.

    b. Schedule II.

    c. Schedule III.

    d. Schedule IV.

27. Schedule II medication must be stored in:

    a. A refrigerator.

    b. A locked safe.

    c. A laminar hood.

    d. The DEA cabinet.

28. How much time does a physician have to provide a written prescription for an "emergency prescription"

    for a Schedule II drug?

    a. 24 hours

    b. 48 hours

    c. 72 hours

    d. 7 days

29. How long is a prescription valid if it has "prn" refills written on it by the physician?

   a. 1 month

   b. 6 months

   c. 1 year from the date the prescription was written

   d. As many as needed

30. What is the maximum number of refills allowed on a prescription of lorazepam if authorized by

   a

   physician?

   a. None

   b. Five

   c. 12

   d. Unlimited

31. How many refills are allowed on C-IV drugs?

   a. 5

   b. 3

   c. 1

   d. 0

32. Which of the following potential hazards are addressed by OSHA regulations?

    a. Exposure to wet surfaces and potential slip and falls.

    b. Exposure to bloodborne pathogens.

    c. Exposure to hazardous chemicals.

    d. All of these potential hazards are addressed by OSHA regulations.

33. What is medication therapy management?

    a. Proper storage and handling of medication

    b. Medication-related advertising that is directed to consumers from drug manufacturers

    c. Medication-related information provided to physicians and other health care professionals by pharmacists

    d. A service or group of services that optimize therapeutic outcomes for individual patients

34. A pharmacist receives a prescription for 40 Percocet tablets, but the pharmacy has only 15 tablets in stock. The patient accepts the 15 tablets. How much time does the pharmacist have to provide the remaining 25 tablets?

    a. 24 hours

    b. 72 hours

    c. 96 hours

    d. 6 months

35. Prescription Monitoring Programs focus is:

I. Administration of controlled substance

II. Dispensing of controlled substance

III. Transportation of controlled substance

IV. Prescribing of controlled substance

a. I and II only

b. II and III only

c. III and IV only

d. II and IV only

36. Which of the following is needed to be labeled on the unit-dose-package?

I. The drug's name

II. The drug's strength

III. The expiration dates

IV. Lot number

a. I and II only

b. II and III only

c. III and IV only

d. I, II, III, and IV only

37. Emergency refills are allowed when:

I. Failure to fill the prescription might result in an interruption of therapy.

II. Pharmacist is unable to reach the prescriber after reasonable effort.

III. Pharmacist is unable to reach the prescriber due to natural disaster.

IV. Failure to fill the prescription might create patient suffering.

a. I and II only

b. II and III only

c. III and IV only

d. I, II, III, and IV

38. Per Federal laws, how long does the pharmacy keep records of schedule II drugs?

a. 2 years

b. 3 years

c. 5 years

d. 7 years

39. The information related to transfer of a prescription maintained by each pharmacy shall at least include:

I. Dispensing date of the prescription.

II. Number of refills remaining.

III. Original date of the prescription.

IV. Number of refills authorized.

a. I and II only

b. II and III only

c. III and IV only

d. I, II, III, and IV

40. According to federal laws, what is the minimum time between an initial and third purchase of schedule V OTC drug?

    a. 24 hours

    b. 48 hours

    c. 72 hours

    d. 120 hours

41. What are the total days of supply of Simvastatin 20 mg prescription that may be dispensed with authorized refills, as long as it doesn't exceed the total quantity authorized by the prescriber?

    a. 30 days

    b. 60 day

    c. 90 days

    d. 120 days

42. Per Federal law what is the quantity limit of schedule II drugs to be dispensed at a time?

a. 30 days

b. 60 days

c. 90 days

d. 120 days

43. A prescription is written for metformin 500 mg tablets BID. How long this prescription should be kept

on file?

a. 6 months

b. 1 year

c. 2 years

d. 3 years

44. How many refills are allowed for Xanax?

a. 3 refills in 6 months

b. 4 refills in 6 months

c. 5 refills in 6 months

d. 6 refills in 5 months

45. If the drug is labeled August 2020, what date does the drug expire?

   a. 08/01/2020

   b. 08/31/2020

   c. 07/01/2020

   d. 07/31/2020

46. What is the maximum day supply of the medication the pharmacy can dispense for an emergency

situation like natural disaster fill?

   a. 10 days

   b. 14 days

   c. 30 days

   d. 60 days

47. Per Federal law if a prescription fails to send a cover prescription for the controlled drug, the pharmacy shall notify the Bureau of Narcotic Enforcement in writing within:

   a. 80 hours of the prescriber's failure to do so.

   b. 120 hours of the prescriber's failure to do so.

   c. 144 hours of the prescriber's failure to do so.

   d. 160 hours of the prescriber's failure to do so.

48. Medicaid/Medicare records of patient's are required to be stored for at least:

a. 5 years

b. 7 years

c. 10 years.

d. 12 years.

49. A prescriber may authorize a maximum of how many refills on a prescription for Percodan tablets?

a. 0

b. 1

c. 2

d. 5

e. 10

50. Which of the following drugs or devices does not require a patient package Insert (PPI)?

I. Conjugated estrogens.

II. Progesterone containing drugs.

III. Intrauterine devices.

IV. Oral contraceptives.

a. II only

b. I and II only

c. I, II, III only

d. I, II, III and IV

51. A prescription for a controlled substance II must include the following information EXCEPT:

a. Patient's name

b. Patient's address

c. DEA registration number

d. Number of refills

52. Which of the following schedule II prescription elements CANNOT be changed with the prescriber's permission?

a. Drug quantity

b. Dosage form

c. Direction of use

d. Drug name

53. An exact count is allowed for schedule IV product in a container that holds greater or equal to ___________ capsules or tablets.

a. 500

b. 1000

c. 1500

d. 2000

54. The prescriber shall keep records of the information on the prescription label for:

a. 2 years

b. 3 years

c. 4 years

d. 5 years

55. According to Federal law, what is the drug classification for Mazindol?

a. Schedule II

b. Schedule III

c. Schedule IV

d. Schedule V

56. DEA form 222 must exclusively contain only these substances EXCEPT:

a. Carfentanil
b. Etorphine HCL
c. Diprenorphine
d. Hydromorphone

57. Per Federal law which of the following may be sold without a prescription?

a. Pregabalin
b. Tramadol
c. Modafinil
d. Robitussin AC

58. A practitioner may dispense directly to ultimate user a controlled substance classified in Schedule II in an amount not to exceed:

a. 48-hours supply
b. 72-hours supply
c. 120-hours supply
d. 180-hours supply

59. All prescription records for non-controlled substances shall be maintained on the licensed premises for a period of ____________________ from the date of dispensing.

a. 1 year

b. 2 years

c. 3 years

d. 4 years

60. What must be found on all controlled substance prescriptions?

a. Pharmacy DEA number

b. Physician's business license number

c. Physician's DEA number

d. Physician's license number

61. A prescription for **Xanax** is valid for:

a. 4 months

b. 5 months

c. 6 months

d. 12 months

62. Which of the following is an example of 3 file storage system?

   a. Schedule I, Schedule II- III, Schedule V

   b. Schedule II, Schedule III-V, Non-scheduled

   c. Schedule I, Schedule II- V, Non-scheduled

   d. Schedule II, Schedule III, Schedule IV, Schedule V

63. If a prescription is written for a 90-day supply, then what is the expiration term for this prescription?

   a. Original plus 2 refills

   b. Original plus 3 refills

   c. Original plus 4 refills

   d. Original plus 11 refills

64. When a pharmacist partially fills controlled substance II, the remaining portion of a schedule II prescription may be filled within:

   a. 24-hours of the first partial filling.

   b. 36-hours of the first partial filling.

   c. 48-hours of the first partial filling.

   d. 72-hours of the first partial filling.

65. What is the schedule for 100 mg of dihydrocodeine in a 100 ml solution (including non-narcotic ingredients)?

   a. Schedule II

   b. Schedule III

   c. Schedule IV

   d. Schedule V

66. Which of the following medications requires an exact count as an inventory?

   a. Soma

   b. Vimpat

   c. Halcion

   d. Percocet

67. A prescription of allopurinol 100 mg, # 180 prescribed for "office use" by Dr. Bilal: What course of action would you take?

   a. Fill the entire prescription

   b. Only fill 30 tablets

   c. Fill after verifying the prescription

   d. Don't fill. Prescription for office use is not acceptable.

68. If a pharmacy partially fills a schedule II prescription, upon each partial fill the pharmacist must document:

I. Date of fill.

II. The quantity dispensed.

III. The remaining quantity.

IV. The pharmacist's sign.

a. I and II only

b. II and III only

c. III and IV only

d. I, II, III, and IV

69. Patient counseling is required for:

I. New prescription pick-up

II. Each medication refills

III. Medicaid patient's prescription

IV. Older than 50 years age

a. I and II only

b. II and III only

c. III and IV only

d. I and III only

70. Which form is used to report lost or stolen drugs?

a. DEA 41

b. DEA 222

c. DEA 224

d. DEA 106

71. Prescription labeling requirement is exempted for:

I. Mail order pharmacy

II. Internet pharmacy

III. Inpatient hospital pharmacy

IV. Outpatient community pharmacy

a. I and II only

b. II and III only

c. III only

d. I, II, III, and IV

72. Which of the following is TRUE about schedule II prescription?

I. It can be refilled.

II. It can be transferred.

III. It can be faxed.

IV. It can be emailed.

a. II only

b. III only

c. IV only

d. None of the above.

73. The partial filling of a schedule II drugs for terminally ill patients must be carried out within:

a. 10 days from the initial filling

b. 96 hours from the initial filling.

c. 30 days from the initial filling.

d. 72 hours from the initial filling

74. The prescriber is mandated to return the hardcopy prescription within __________ days after giving over the phone schedule II emergency supply per Federal law.

a. 24 hours

b. 72 hours

c. 7 days

d. 10 days

75. What is the maximum number of control substances that can be imported by the individuals into the United States?

   a. 30 dosage units

   b. 50 dosage units

   c. 90 dosage units

   d. 120 dosage units

PART TWO

NEVADA PHARMACY LAW ANSWERS

1. Answer: D

   The minimum age of a purchaser is not addressed under Nevada laws.

2. Answer: D

   It is required to collect up to 1740 practical experience hours.

3. Answer: C

   The successful completion of at least 1,500 hours of training and experience is required by pharmacy technicians.

4. Answer: (b)

   Schedule II controlled prescriptions for patients in LTCF or patients with a medical diagnosis documenting a terminal illness are valid for a period not to exceed 60 days from the issue date.

5. Answer: D

   The remaining portion of schedule II prescription may be filled within 72 hours after the first partial filling. If the remaining portion is not or cannot be filled within the 72-hour period, the pharmacist shall notify the prescribing practitioner.

6. Answer: B

   A facsimile prescription of schedule III drug received by the pharmacy must be kept by the pharmacist for at least 2 years after it is received by him.

7. Answer: B

   In Nevada, the inventory of controlled substances should be done every 2 years.

8. Answer: B

According to Nevada State Pharmacy Law, inventory records must be maintained for a period of at least two years from the date of such inventory or record.

9. Answer: C

A pharmacist must complete 30 hours of continuing education biennially in order to renew his/her license.

10. Answer: D

An emergency oral prescription for Schedule II controlled drugs must be mailed to dispensing pharmacy by an authorized prescriber within 72 hours after an oral authorization.

11. Answer: B

Governor, [Nevada Revised Statues-639.030].

The Governor shall appoint:

(a). Six members who are registered pharmacists in the State of Nevada, are actively engaged in the practice of pharmacy in the State of Nevada and have had at least 5 years of experience as registered pharmacists preceding the appointment.

(b). One member who is a representative of the general public and is not related to a pharmacist registered in the State of Nevada by consanguinity or affinity within the third degree.

2. Appointments of registered pharmacists must be representative of the practice of pharmacy.

3. Within 30 days after appointment, each member of the Board shall take and subscribe an oath to discharge faithfully and impartially the duties prescribed by this chapter.

4. After the initial terms, the members of the Board must be appointed to terms of 3 years. A person may not serve as a member of the Board for more than three consecutive terms.

If a vacancy occurs during a member's term, the Governor shall appoint a person qualified under this section to replace that member for the remainder of the unexpired term.

5. The Governor shall remove from the Board any member, after a hearing, for neglect of duty or other just cause.

12. Answer: A

14 days. Exception: where a C-2 prescription has a future fill, or "do not fill until" date , the 14 days begins on the day after the future fill or "do not fill until" date.

13. Answer: A

The "do not fill date" must not be later than 3 months after the date the prescription was written. If the RX was written on Jan 1, the latest "do not fill date" is April 1.

14. Answer: C

90 days.

15. Answer: B

90 MME. Additionally the medication must be intended to be used for no more than 14 days

16. Answer: B

3 technicians. Pharmaceutical technicians-in-training count against this ratio, but interns do not.

17. Answer: B

The Controlled Substances Act allows for the partial filling of a Schedule II medication prescription, with the remaining medication to be provided to the patient within 72 hours or the quantity becomes void.

18. Answer: A

The first letter of a physician's DEA number will be A, B, F, or M. The second letter is the first letter of the physician's last name at the time he or she applied for the DEA number. DEA numbers are required as a result of the Controlled Substances Act.

19. Answer: B

On discovery of a theft of controlled sub- stances, the local law enforcement agency must be notified, and DEA Form 106 needs to be submitted.

20. Answer: A

A class I drug recall may cause irreversible injury or possibly death to a patient, a class II drug recall may cause reversible harm to the patient, and a class III drug recall does not cause injury to the patient.

21. Answer: C

USP, 795. Addresses no sterile compounding, and USP, 797. Deals with sterile compounding.

22. Answer: B

Under the Combat Methamphetamine Epidemic Act of 2005, the maximum amount of pseudoephedrine that may purchase in a single day is 3.6 g; the maximum amount that may be purchased in a 30-day time period is 9 g.

23. Answer: C

The Controlled Substances Act specifies that a DEA permit is valid for 3 years.

24. Answer: C

Form 222 is a triplicate order form for schedule 1 and 2 controlled substances. The purchaser submits copy 1 and 2 to the supplier and keeps copy 3 on file.

25. Answer: D

The Red Book is the leading resource for information on drug pricing.

26. Answer: A

Schedule I includes drugs such as Marijuana, Ecstasy, Peyote, and Heroin.

27. Answer: B

All schedule II substances should be stored in a locked safe, while schedule III, IV and V may be stored throughout the pharmacy.

28. Answer: D

According to the Controlled Substances Act, a physician has up to 7 calendar days to provide a pharmacy a handwritten prescription for a Sched- ule II medication if it was called in to the pharmacy. The quantity prescribed should be enough to last only until the patient can see the physician.

29. Answer: C

Although the expression "prn" means as needed, a prescription with "prn" refills can only be refilled

up to 1 year from the date the medication was prescribed.

Any additional refills require the prescriber's approval.

30. Answer: B

Lorazepam is classified as a Schedule IV medication under the Controlled Substance Act and is permitted to be refilled a maximum of five times within 6 months of the prescription's being written.

31. Answer: A

CIII drugs can have up to 5 refills and are refillable up to 6 months. Some examples of C-IV drugs include Xanax.

32. Answer: D

OSHA regulations address the following potential hazards in a pharmacy: Exposure to bloodborne pathogens (HIV, Hepatitis B & C), exposure to hazardous chemicals or drugs, exposure of eyes or bodies to corrosive materials, exposure to latex allergy, exposure to wet surfaces that could cause slip and falls, and availability of personal protective equipment.

33. Answer: D

Medication storage and handling, as well as both consumer and professional information, may be parts of medication therapy management, but the more comprehensive definition of a service or group of services that optimize therapeutic outcomes for individual patients is the best answer.

34. Answer: B

The Controlled Substances Act allows for the partial filling of a Schedule II medication prescription, with the remaining medication to be provided to the patient within 72 hours or the quantity becomes void.

35. Answer: D

Prescription Monitoring Programs focus is dispensing and prescribing of controlled substance.

36. Answer: D

Unit-dose-package label include:

- The drug's name
- The drug's strength
- The expiration dates
- Lot number

37. Answer: D

All the above conditions may qualify to refill emergency prescription.

38. Answer: A

Per Federal laws, the pharmacy keeps records of schedule II drugs for 2 years

39. Answer: D

The information related to transfer of a prescription maintained by each pharmacy shall at least include:

- Dispensing date of the prescription.
- Number of refills remaining.
- Original date of the prescription.
- Number of refills authorized.

40. Answer: B

According to federal laws, it is 48 hours.

41. Answer: C

A pharmacy may dispense accelerated refills of up to a 90-day supply of medication pursuant to a valid prescription that may be dispensed with authorized refills, as long as it doesn't exceed the total quantity authorized by the prescriber.

42. Answer: C

There is 90-day supply limit to all schedule II drugs per federal laws.

43. Answer: B

Metformin is a legend drug, and the prescription should be kept on file for 2 years.

44. Answer: C

Xanax is classified as controlled substances (schedule IV).

45. Answer: B

The drug expires the last day of the month.

46. Answer: C

The maximum day supply of the medication the pharmacy can dispense for an emergency situation like natural disaster fill is 30 days' supply.

47. Answer: C

If a prescription fails to send a cover prescription for the controlled drug, the pharmacy shall notify the Bureau of Narcotic Enforcement in writing within 144 hours of the prescriber's failure to do so.

48. Answer is C

Records related to Medicaid/Medicare patients are required to be stored for at least.

10 ears.

49. Answer: A

Schedule II drugs has no refills.

50. Answer: D

All the above drugs or devices does not require a patient package Insert (PPI).

51. Answer: D

C-II prescriptions don't have refills.

52. Answer: D

Following elements of schedule II prescription cannot be changed/added:

- Patient's name
- Drug name
- Prescriber's name
- Prescriber's signature

53. Answer: B

An exact count is allowed for schedule III- V products in a container that holds greater or equal to 1000 capsules or tablets.

54. Answer: B

The prescriber shall keep records of the information on the prescription label for 3 years.

55. Answer: C

Mazindol – Schedule IV drug per Federal law

56. Answer: D

Hydromorphone can be mentioned on DEA form 222 with other drugs. But not carfentanil, etorphine HCL, and diprenorphine.

57. Answer: D

Per Federal law Robitussin AC may be sold without a prescription.

58. Answer: B

A practitioner may dispense directly to un ultimate user a controlled substance classified in Schedule II in an amount not to exceed 72-hours supply.

59. Answer: A

All prescription records for non-controlled substances shall be maintained on the licensed premises for a period of one year from the date of dispensing.

60. Answer: C

The Controlled Substances Act requires that all prescribers and dispensers of controlled sub- stances have a DEA number. The requirement shows the pharmacist that the physician has the authority to prescribe controlled substances.

61. Answer: C

A prescription for schedule III to IV is valid for 6 months.

62. Answer: B

3 file storage system means: Schedule II, Schedule III-V, Non-scheduled.

63. Answer: B

90 days = 1 months plus 3 refills

64. Answer: D

When a pharmacist partially fills controlled substance II, the remaining portion of a schedule II prescription may be filled within 72-hours of the first partial filling.

65. Answer: D

100 mg/100 ml of dihydrocodeine solution is a schedule V drug.

66. Answer: D

Schedule II drug Percocet requires an exact count for inventory.

67. Answer: D

The prescription should not be filled because a prescription is the incorrect method to order drugs "for office use."

68. Answer: D

The pharmacist must document upon each partial fill:

- Date of fill.
- The quantity dispensed.
- The remaining quantity.
- The pharmacist's sign.

69. Answer: D

Patient counseling is required for new prescription pick-up and Medicaid patient's prescription.

70. Answer: D

Stolen medications reported via DEA form 106.

71. Answer: C

Prescription labeling requirement is exempted for inpatient hospital pharmacy.

72. Answer: D

It cannot be refilled, transferred or faxed it can be faxed only on few exceptions.

73. Answer: B

An opioid treatment program certification shall be granted for a term not to exceed 3 years.

74. Answer: C

The prescriber is mandated to return the hardcopy prescription within SEVEN days after giving over the phone schedule II emergency supply.

75. Answer: B

Individuals may not import more than 50 dosage units of control substance medications into the United States from any foreign country.

REFERENCES

1. DEA's Diversion Control Division Website www.DEAdiversion.usdoj.gov
2. DEA Homepage www.dea.gov
3. U.S. Government Publishing Office
4. https://www.govinfo.gov Provides access to the CFR, Parts 1300 to End, primary source for the Pharmacist's Manual, and the Federal Register which contains proposed and finalized amendments to the CFR.
5. Office of National Drug Control Policy (ONDCP) www.whitehouse.gov/ondcp
6. Food and Drug Administration www.FDA.gov
7. SAMHSA www.samhsa.gov
8. CSAT https://www.samhsa.gov/about-us/who-we-are/offices-centers/csat
9. Federation of State Medical Boards www.FSMB.org
10. National Association of Boards of Pharmacy https://nabp.pharmacy
11. National Association of State Controlled Substances Authorities www.nascsa.org

Made in the USA
Las Vegas, NV
15 April 2025

20993989R00063